Introduction

Shooting is a central component of team handball and must be practiced and improved regularly. Therefore, it is reasonable to integrate shooting series into training units from time to time. This collection of exercises contains 60 comprehensible practical drills focusing on this subject. They can be integrated in every training unit.

The exercises are divided into the following six categories and three difficulty levels (easy, medium, difficult):
- Technique
- Shooting at fixed targets
- Series of shots at the goal
- Shooting training for specific playing positions
- Complex series of shots
- Shooting competitions

With these options, you can easily make your shooting trainings more diverse and create new approaches for every age group. Additional notes and possible variations should inspire you to further modify the exercises and to adjust them to your players' level of performance.

Sample figure:

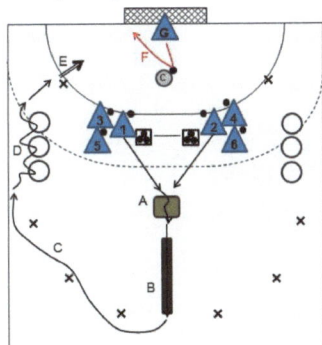

1st English edition released on 16.03.2016
German original edition released on 04 Nov 2015

Published by DV Concept
Editors, Design and Layout: Jörg Madinger, Elke Lackner
Proofreading and English translation: Nina-Maria Nahlenz

ISBN: 978-3-95641-166-3

The book and its contents are protected by copyright. No reprinting, photomechanical reproduction, storing or processing in electronic systems without the publisher's written permission.

Contents:

No.	Name	Players	Difficulty level	Page
Category: Technique				
1	Wrist technique	2	⭐	6
2	Passing and shooting technique	2	⭐	7
Category: Shooting at fixed targets				
3	Shooting at medicine balls	8	⭐	9
4	Drill: Shooting at different targets	8	⭐	10
5	Shooting at targets	8	⭐	12
6	Competition: Shooting at fixed targets	8	⭐	13
7	Shooting at targets defined by playing cards	9	⭐	14
8	Shooting at fixed targets in the goal	6	⭐⭐	15
Category: Series of shots at the goal				
9	Continuous shooting from different positions	6	⭐	16
10	Series of shots at defined targets	7	⭐	17
11	Series of shots with coordination exercise	7	⭐	18
12	Series of shots with simple crossing	6	⭐⭐	19
13	Series of shots on several positions with defense	7	⭐⭐	20
14	Series of shots with previous coordination exercise	6	⭐⭐	21
15	Series of shots with previous exercise and fast break	11	⭐⭐	22
16	Series of shots at defined corners	7	⭐⭐	23
17	Series of shots with previous reaction exercise	7	⭐⭐	24
18	Series of shots with two variants and decision-making	10	⭐⭐	25
19	Series of shots with coordination and passing	7	⭐⭐	27
20	Series of shots with defensive block and fast break	9	⭐⭐	28
21	Series of shots with penalties	6	⭐⭐	29
22	Series of shots with previous coordination exercise and consecutive action	9	⭐⭐⭐	30
23	Shooting during endurance training	8	⭐⭐⭐	31
24	Series of shots with athletics drill	11	⭐⭐⭐	32

No.	Name	Players	Difficulty level	Page
Category: Shooting training for specific playing positions				
25	Shooting from individual positions 1	3	★	33
26	Shooting from positions with coordination run	3	★	35
27	Series of shots for the wing players with previous exertion	8	★	36
28	Series of shots for the back position players	3	★	37
29	Series of shots for the CB player	6	★	38
30	Series of shots for the pivot	5	★	39
31	Series of shots for the wing players 2	6	★★	40
32	Series of shots for the LB and RB players with exertion	9	★★	41
33	Series of shots for the back positions and running moves without the ball	8	★★	42
34	Series of shots for the pivot 2	6	★★	43
35	Series of shots from the back positions with block	6	★★	44
36	Series of shots with decision-making on the back and wing positions	8	★★	45
37	Shooting circle training for specific playing positions	8	★★	47
38	Series of shots for the back positions with crossing 1	10	★★	48
39	Series of shots for the back positions with crossing 2	7	★★	49
40	Series of shots for the wing players with crossing on the back positions	8	★★	50
Category: Complex series of shots				
41	Series of shots with previous exercise	3	★★	51
42	Initial actions as series of shots from different positions	10	★★	52
43	All-position shooting with defense	12	★★	54
44	Shooting with consecutive 1-on-1 fast break	8	★★	56
45	Two shots over the block with consecutive fast break	10	★★	57
46	Shooting in the 1st wave with previous exercise	5	★★	58
47	Series of shots with undetermined situations	9	★★★	59
48	Series of shots with coordination and passing exercise	8	★★★	60
49	Series of shots with athletics drill and defense	9	★★★	61
50	Series of shots with four 1-on-1 actions	10	★★★	62

No.	Name	Players	Difficulty level	Page
Category: Shooting competitions				
51	Shooting competition with game of pairs	9	★	63
52	Shooting competition with medicine balls	6	★	64
53	Shooting competition with dices	7	★	65
54	Shooting competition timed by the other group 1	9	★	66
55	Shooting competition timed by the other group 2	9	★★	67
56	Shooting at fixed targets vs. shooting at the goal	9	★★	68
57	Shooting biathlon	10	★★	70
58	Fast break shooting competition	8	★★	71
59	Shooting competition focusing on endurance	8	★★★	72
60	Sprint-and-shoot relay race with dices	12	★★★	73

Editor's note

Further reference books published by DV Concept

Varied handball shooting drills
60 exercises for every handball training unit

Key:

No. of exercise — Name of exercise — Minimum number of players

No. 3	**Shooting at medicine balls**	8	⭐
Equipment required:	4 small vaulting boxes, 4 medicine balls, 8 cones, sufficient number of handballs		

Difficulty level
Easy: ⭐
Medium: ⭐⭐
Difficult: ⭐⭐⭐

✖ Cone

Ball box

Small gym mat

Large vaulting box

Small vaulting box

Small vaulting box, upside down

Hoop

Balance bench

Coordination ladder

Dice

Medicine ball / tennis ball

Pole

Hurdle

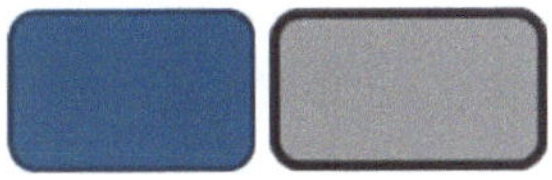

Large safety mat

Category: Technique

No. 1	Wrist technique	2	★
Equipment required:	1 handball per player		

Setting:
- Two players, each holding a handball, stand face-to-face at a distance of about 4 to 5 meters.
- Both players do the exercise in parallel.

Preparation:
- Before starting the exercise, the players should rotate their wrists (clockwise and counterclockwise), hinge them back and forth, and finally stretch them slightly.

(Figure 1)

Course 1:
- The players lift their arms to the side at an angle of 90°, hinge the wrist back as far as possible (figure 1), and pass the ball to the other player by only moving their wrists (figure 2).
- Change the throwing hand after 20 to 30 passes.

(Figure 2)

⚠ The players should pass the ball in such a way that their teammate can catch it at chest height.

Course 2:
- The players lift their arms straight up, hinge back their wrists (figure 3), and pass the ball to the other player by only moving the wrist. The players should hinge their wrists back (figure 3) and forth (figure 4) as far as possible.

(Figure 3) (Figure 4)

Course 3:
- The players hold their arms down and to the side, hinge their wrists back as far as possible (figure 5), and pass the ball to the other player by only moving their wrists (figure 6).

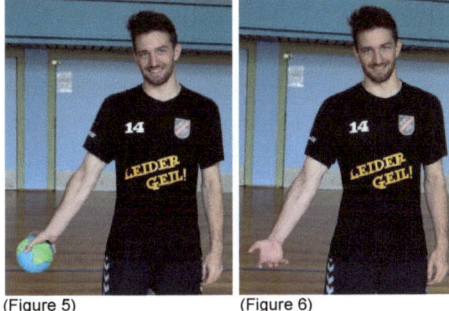
(Figure 5)   (Figure 6)

⚠ The pass should be played by only moving the wrist – this applies to each of the three arm positions; the arm must not be moved but rather kept in the respective position.

No. 2	Passing and shooting technique	2	★
Equipment required:	1 handball per team of two, 6 cones, large vaulting box, balance bench, 3 medicine balls		

Setting of course 1:
- Two players stand face-to-face, each pair having one handball.

Course 1:
- The players keep passing the ball while moving back and forth (A and B).

Variant:
- The players run a slight curve to the left (right) (C) and then pass the ball to their teammate (D).

⚠ Make sure that the toes point towards the teammate while passing the ball.

Course 2:
- The players shoot at medicine balls on top of a balance bench (E).

Course 3:
- The players shoot at cones on top of a large vaulting box (F).

Course 4:
- The players shoot at cones on the floor (G).

Observe the following:

⚠️ The right-handed player moves forward and plants his left foot firmly on the ground observing the three-step rule. His toes must point towards the teammate (shooting target) (figure 1). For left-handed players, the movement is done the other way around.

(Figure 1)   (Figure 2)

⚠️ The hip and upper body are rotated backwards. The upper arm and elbow must be in line with the shoulder (figure 1).

⚠️ The players must keep their elbows up while moving forward. The hip and upper body are rotated forward (figure 2).

⚠️ The players must move the backmost foot forward and rotate the arm forward as well (while keeping the elbow up however) in order to get a smooth rotation movement (hip, upper body, and arm) (figure 3).

⚠️ The backmost foot moves forward, the arm swings forward, and finally the ball is being passed to the teammate (shot at the target) by hinging the wrist (figure 4).

(Figure 3)   (Figure 4)

Category: Shooting at fixed targets

No. 3	Shooting at medicine balls	8	★
Equipment required:	4 small vaulting boxes, 4 medicine balls, 8 cones, sufficient number of handballs		

Setting:
- The players form pairs. Each team of 2 gets a small vaulting box with a medicine ball on top that serves as the target. Define the shooting distance with two cones.

Course 1:
- 1 starts as the shooter, 2 starts as the feeder.
- 2 plays three passes to 1 (A).
- 1 makes a well-controlled rotation movement and shoots (B).
- 1 tries to hit the medicine ball.
- Switch tasks after three shots.
- The other groups do the drill in parallel.
- Repeat the drill four times until each player has shot 12 times.

Course 2:
- The basic course remains the same as course 1.
- The shooters shoot three times – from the front center (B), from next to the left cone, and from next to the right cone (C) in order to change the shooting angle.

⚠ Make sure that the shooting movement is performed correctly (rotate hip and body backwards, elbow in line with the head/shoulder, body rotation, target focus, toes point towards the shooting direction).

Varied handball shooting drills
60 exercises for every handball training unit

No. 4	Drill: Shooting at different targets	8	★
Equipment required:	2 small vaulting boxes, 1 large vaulting box, 1 balance bench, 1 large safety mat, tape, 9 cones, 2 ropes or hoops, 1 handball per player		

Overall course:
- The course consists of several exercises and must be done twice.
- The players do the exercises in groups (no more than 4 players per group).
- The exercises are changed on command after a defined time period.

Exercise 1:
- Put two small vaulting boxes into the goal and attach targets to the upper goal corners, such as ropes or hoops.
- The players run a few meters, shoot and try to hit one of the four targets in the goal (A).

Exercise 2:
- Position a large safety mat upright on the wall. Define several individual fields on the mat using white or colored tape. Also define a shooting line in front of the mat from which the players are allowed to shoot.
- The players shoot alternately and try to hit each field consecutively (B).
- Who hits each field at least once first?

Exercise 3:
- Build up a large vaulting box and draw a circle around it.
- The players try to hit the individual parts of the vaulting box consecutively from outside the circle, first on the long side (C), then on the short side (D).

Exercise 4:
- Array cones on top of a balance bench. Define a shooting line in front of the bench from which the players are allowed to shoot.
- Both players shoot alternately and try to hit the cones (E).
- Who hits more often?

⚠ Make sure the players perform the shooting and passing movements correctly.

⚠ Adjust the target distance and the shooting variants to the players' level of performance.

⚠ The exercises are also suitable for video analysis – the players can be shown their mistakes on the computer immediately after the drill.

Varied handball shooting drills
60 exercises for every handball training unit

No. 5	Shooting at targets	8	★
Equipment required:	6 cones, 4 small vaulting boxes, 2 large vaulting boxes, 4 medicine balls, 2 ball boxes with sufficient number of handballs, 2 score cards, 2 pens		

Setting:
- Make two teams; each team gets a score card and a pen.
- For each team, position two medicine balls, two small vaulting boxes, and one large vaulting box as targets. Define shooting lines using cones (see figure).

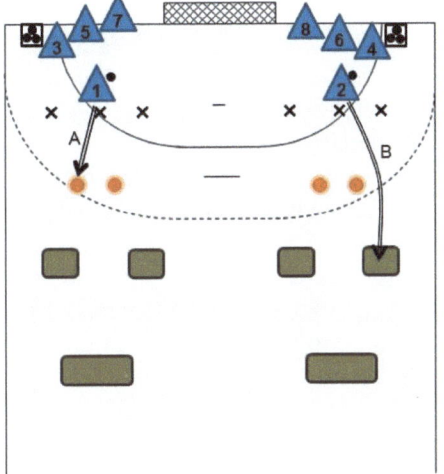

Course:
- ▲1 and ▲2 start with a ball and shoot from the shooting line.
- They either try to hit a medicine ball (A), a small vaulting box (B), or the large vaulting box.
- Once they have hit one of the targets, the respective item may be crossed out on the score card (M for medicine ball, B for the small vaulting box, LB for the large vaulting box).
- The player who has shot runs back and exchanges a high-five with the player who is next in line.
- If the team wishes, they may put the medicine balls back into their original position after a hit.
- Which team is first to hit all the targets on the score card (or has scored highest at the end of the playing time)?

⚠ Make sure that the players do the shooting movements correctly.

⚠ The teams may decide who shoots at which target in order to develop a strategy.

Score card: M: medicine ball, B: small vaulting box, LB: large vaulting box

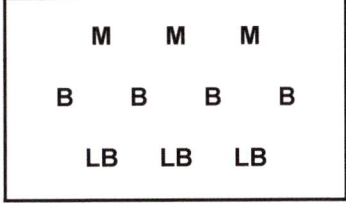

No. 6	Competition: Shooting at fixed targets	8	★
Equipment required:	10 cones, 6 small vaulting boxes, 2 medicine balls, 2 foam dices, 2 ball boxes with sufficient number of handballs		

Setting:

- Make two teams. For each team, position three small vaulting boxes and define a shooting line using cones (see figure).
- Put a medicine ball each on top of the two first boxes, a foam dice each on top of the two second boxes (if no dices are available, use cones or medicine balls), and a cone each on top of the two last boxes.

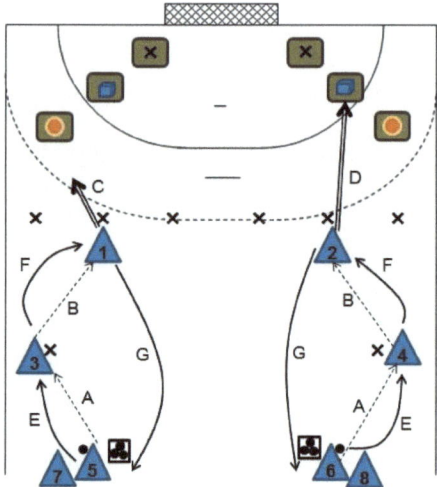

Course:

- On command, 5 and 6 start and play a pass to 3 and 4, respectively (A).
- 3 and 4 pass the ball to 1 and 2, respectively (B).
- 1 and 2 choose a target and shoot (C and D).
- When hitting a target, the players receive points as follows:
    o Medicine ball: 2 points
    o Dice: number of points on the dice after it has been hit
    o Cone: 5 points
- The coach writes down the points of each team. The targets that have been hit must be put back on top of the boxes.
- After they have played the pass, the players take over the position to which they passed the ball (E and F).
- 7 and 8 play the next pass.
- After they have shot, 1 and 2 line up next to the respective ball box (G).
- Each player must shoot 5 (10) times. The team with the most points wins the game.
- Consider a second round.

Variant:

- Limit the playing time. Which team has scored highest after 5 (7) minutes?

⚠ Make sure the players perform the shooting and passing movements correctly. Revise constantly.

⚠ The players may be given some time before the game in order to develop a team strategy.

⚠ If no foam dice is available, the players may shoot at a cone or a medicine ball instead. Once they have hit the respective target, the team may roll a small dice to figure out the number of points.

No. 7	Shooting at targets defined by playing cards	9	★
Equipment required:	11 cones, 4 small vaulting boxes, 3 medicine balls, 1 balance bench, 1 deck of playing cards		

Setting:
- Array cones on top of a balance bench and define a shooting line.
- Position three small vaulting boxes on the opposite, put a medicine ball each on top, and define a shooting line.
- Put a deck of playing cards upside down on top of the small vaulting box at the center line.

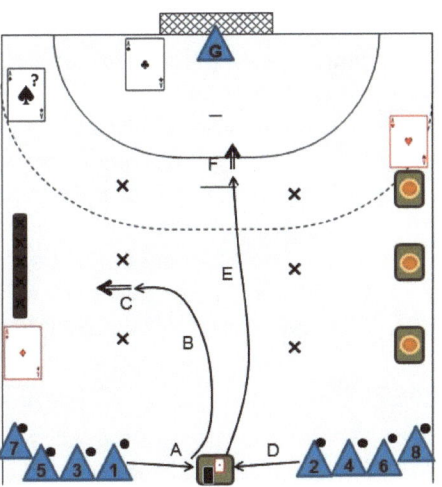

Course:
- There are three shooting targets, of which each is assigned one card suit:
    o Cones on the bench (Diamonds)
    o Medicine balls (Hearts)
    o Goal (Clubs)
- For Spades, the players may choose the shooting target.
- Make two teams. The teams stand on the right and left side of the backmost vaulting box.
- ▲1 starts, flips a card (here Diamonds) (A), runs to the respective shooting line (B), and shoots at the respective target (C).
- If the player hits the target, he gets a point.
- As soon as ▲1 runs to the shooting target, ▲2 starts, flips a card (D) (here Clubs), runs to the shooting line (here the 6-meter line) (E), and shoots (F).
- And so on. Which team scores highest?

No. 8	Shooting at fixed targets inside the goal	6	★★
Equipment required:	4 small vaulting boxes, 2 bibs, 1 handball per player		

Setting:
- Put a small vaulting box next to each goalpost.
- Pile up 2 to 3 small vaulting boxes in the center of the goal.
- Tie a bib each on the left and right side of the crossbar so that it hangs down into the goal.

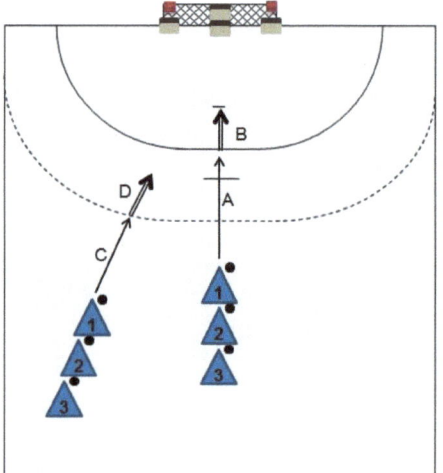

Course 1:
- ▲1 starts to run with the ball and shoots, while running, from the 6-meter line at one of the targets in the goal (A and B).
    - If he hits the 2 to 3 small vaulting boxes in the center of the goal, he gets 1 point.
    - If he hits one of the two small vaulting boxes next to the goalposts, he gets 2 points.
    - If he hits one of the bibs, he gets 3 points.
- Afterwards, it is the next players' turn.
- Who has scored highest after 10 shots?

Course 2:
- ▲1 starts to run with the ball and makes a jump shot from the 9-meter line at one of the targets in the goal (C and D).

⚠ The players should perform the shooting movement correctly.

Category: Series of shots at the goal

| No. 9 | Continuous shooting from different positions | 6 | ★ |

Equipment required: 10 cones, ball box with sufficient number of handballs

Setting:
- Position cones as shown in the figure.

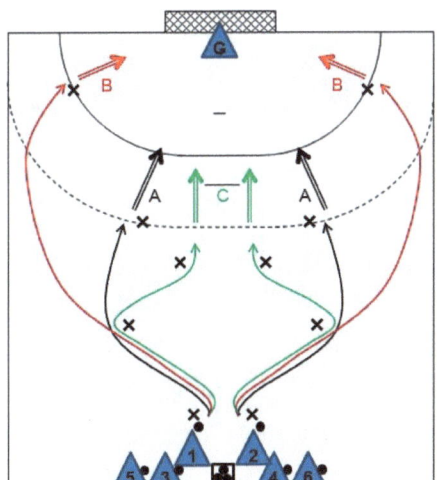

Course A:
- 1 starts from the center, dribbles around the left cone, and makes a jump shot at the goal from the back position (here LB).
- Immediately before 1 shoots at the goal, 2 starts, dribbles around the right cone, and also makes a jump shot at the goal.
- 3 starts slightly delayed and does the same drill.
- After they have shot, the players run back to the starting point as fast as possible (they should pick up the handballs lying around) and repeat the drill until no handballs are left in the ball box (about 25 to 30 shots).

Course B:
- 1 starts from the center, dribbles around the left cone, keeps dribbling until he arrives the wing position, and shoots.
- Since the goalkeeper must cover a longer distance now, 2 must time his start accordingly (by the time the player shoots, the goalkeeper should be in a proper position).
- Repeat until no handballs are left or until the players have shot 25 to 30 times.

Course C:
- 1 starts from the center, dribbles around the left cone, dynamically dribbles towards the center, and makes a jump shot.
- Immediately before 1 shoots, 2 starts the same drill.
- Repeat until no handballs are left or until the players have shot 25 to 30 times.

⚠ The players should run around the cones and approach the goal in a highly dynamic manner.

No. 10	Series of shots at defined targets	7	★
Equipment required:	1 large vaulting box, 2 cones, 1 deck of playing cards, 1 handball per player		

Setting:
- Put two piles of cards upside down on top of the large vaulting box.
- The shooting corridor is defined with two cones.
- Each card suit is assigned a goal corner.

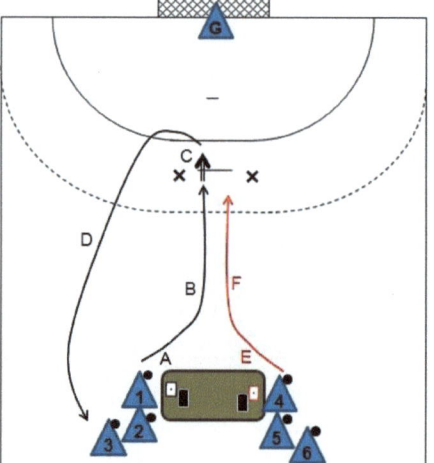

Course:
- **1** starts and flips the first card (A).
- **1** dribbles towards the cones and shoots at the goal (B and C).
- **1** tries to hit the corner assigned to the card suit.

If **1** succeeds, he gets three points for his team. If **1** hits one of the other corners, he gets one point for his team. If he does not hit the goal at all, he does not get a point.

- Afterwards, **1** runs back to his team (D) and **4** starts (E and F).

Competition:
- Which team gets the most points with their pile of cards?

Varied handball shooting drills
60 exercises for every handball training unit

No. 11	Series of shots with coordination exercise	7	★
Equipment required:	8 cones, 1 balance bench, 6 hoops, 1 small vaulting box, 2 ball boxes with sufficient number of handballs		

Setting:
- Position the small vaulting box, bench, hoops, and cones as shown in the figure.
- Make two teams (shooters left and right). Each team has a ball box containing the same number of handballs.

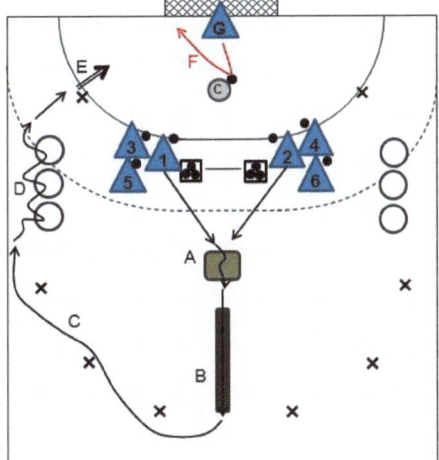

Course:
- ① starts with a ball, dribbles towards the small vaulting box, and crosses it, still dribbling (A). Then he crosses the bench while bouncing the ball on the floor next to the bench (B).
- ① dribbles a slalom around the cones (C), bounces the ball into each hoop once (D), picks up the ball, and shoots from the left wing position (E).
- Once ① has arrived the hoops, the goalkeeper runs towards the coach, touches the handball the coach is holding, and finally gets in position for the shot from the wing position (F).
- If ① scores, he fetches the ball and puts it into the ball box of the other team. If ① misses, he puts the ball into his own team's ball box. ① lines up again.
- ② starts the same drill once ① has left the bench; however, after crossing the bench, he runs to the right side and shoots from the right wing position.
- Which team has fewer handballs in their box after the time is up?

⚠ The players should do the coordination exercises in a concentrated manner and – if possible – without making mistakes; the players should speed up only after they have gained more and more confidence.

⚠ The coach holds the handball for the goalkeeper (F) in different positions – up, down, left, or right so that the goalkeeper must react accordingly.

⚠ Consider playing two rounds and changing the sides.

| No. 12 | Series of shots with simple crossing | 6 | ★★ |

Equipment required: 2 cones, ball box with sufficient number of handballs

Setting:
- Position cones as shown in the figure.

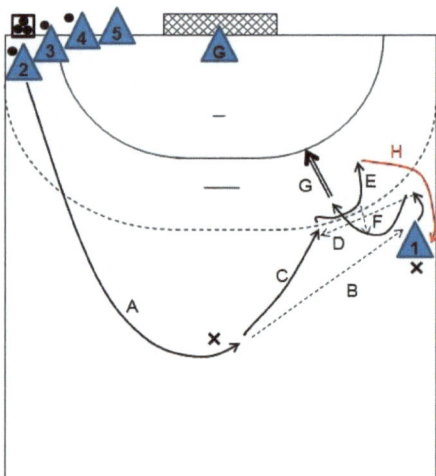

Course:
- 2 dribbles to the cone (A).
- Once he has arrived at the cone, 2 passes the ball to 1 (B) and keeps running (C).
- 1 makes a slight piston movement and passes the ball into the running path of 2 (D).
- 2 starts crossing (E), 1 takes on the crossing, receives the pass (F), and shoots (G).
- 2 immediately moves back to the position of 1 (H) while 3 dribbles towards him and starts the next round.
- 1 lines up again with a ball.
- After several rounds, start the course over from the other side so that the players shoot from the LB position.

⚠ The players should start the crossing dynamically, take it on at full speed, and shoot.

⚠ The next player starts in time so that the previous player must catch the ball (B) immediately after he has moved back to the cone (H).

Varied handball shooting drills
60 exercises for every handball training unit

No. 13	Series of shots on several positions with defense	7	★★
Equipment required:	8 cones, ball box with sufficient number of handballs		

Setting:
- Position cones as shown in the figure.
- 2 and 3 feed 1 who does a series of five actions.

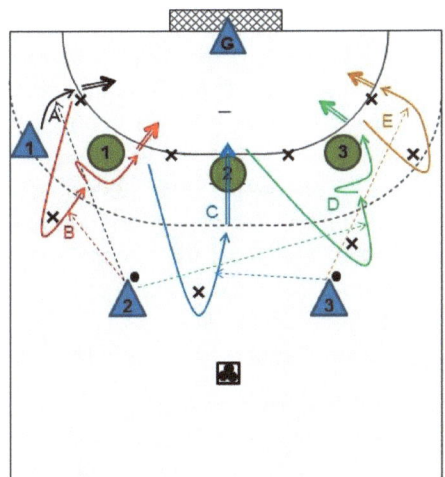

Course:
- **Action 1:** 1 receives a pass from 2 to the left wing position into his running path and shoots (A).
- **Action 2:** After the 1st shot, 1 moves back immediately and runs around the 1st cone. Afterwards, he receives a pass into his running path (B), plays 1-on-1 against 1, and finally shoots at the goal.
- **Action 3:** After the action, 1 immediately moves back and runs around the 2nd cone. Afterwards, he receives a pass into his running path (C) and makes a jump shot over 2 who serves as defensive block.
- **Action 4:** After the action, 1 immediately moves back and runs around the 3rd cone. Afterwards, he receives a pass into his running path (D), plays 1-on-1 against 3, and finally shoots at the goal.
- **Action 5:** After the action, 1 immediately moves back and runs around the 4th cone. He subsequently receives a pass to the right wing position into his running path (E) and shoots.

Subsequent course:
- The other players fetch the balls so that there is no break between the shots.
- After the last shot, the players (also the players who have fetched the balls) move on to the next position: e.g., 1 becomes 1, 3 becomes 3, 3 becomes 2, 1 becomes the feeder or fetches the balls, etc. The players move on to the next position clockwise.

Varied handball shooting drills
60 exercises for every handball training unit

No. 14	Series of shots with previous coordination exercise	6	★★
Equipment required:	1 coordination ladder, 1 handball per player		

Course 1:
- ![1] jumps through the coordination ladder while doing jumping jacks and holding a ball. He jumps with both legs into the first interspace (A), afterwards he jumps and lands with his feet on the left and right side of the coordination ladder (B), etc., until he arrives at the end of the ladder.
- When landing with both legs for the last time, ![1] jumps forward and upwards with both legs (C) and shoots at the goal (jump shot) (D).
- Afterwards, ![2] starts the same drill.

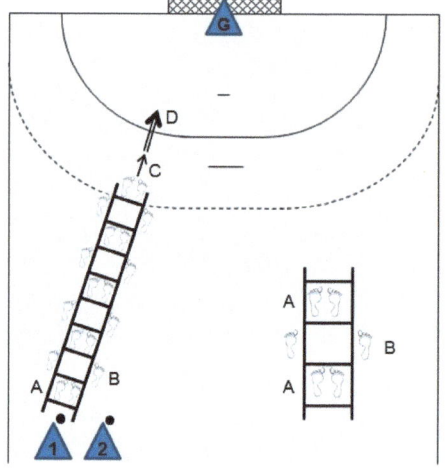

⚠ Make sure that the players do the jumping jacks in the coordination ladder quickly.

Course 2:
- ![1] runs through the coordination ladder as fast as possible with 2 footsteps per interspace (E).
- At the end, ![1] makes three quick steps (without dribbling) straight towards the center (shooting angle as good as possible) (F) and makes a jump shot at the goal (G).

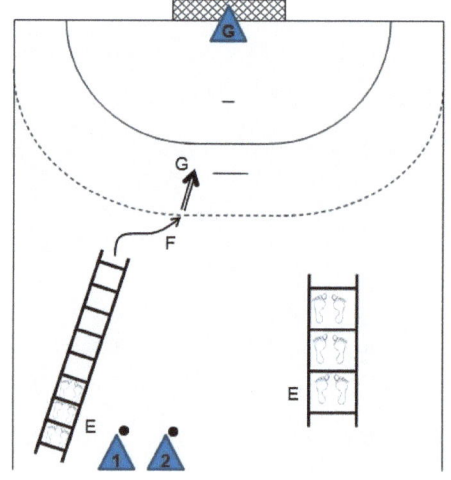

Varied handball shooting drills
60 exercises for every handball training unit

No. 15	Series of shots with previous exercise and fast break	11	★★
Equipment required:	2 large safety mats, 3 cones		

Setting:
- Position the large safety mats on the floor along the center line and define the running paths with cones (see figure).

Course:
- 1 starts and does 10 quick jumping jacks in front of the large safety mat.
- Afterwards, 1 does 10 fast high-knees (in place) (A) on the safety mat while holding his handball.
- 1 passes the ball to the coach (B), sprints around the cone, receives a return pass (C), and makes a jump shot from the 9-meter line (D).
- After his shot, 1 starts a fast break immediately (E).
- G2 passes the ball into the running path of 1 once he has crossed the center line (F).
- 1 makes a jump shot (G), fetches his ball quickly, and lines up on the other side (H).
- Once 1 has stepped on the safety mat (A), 2 starts to do 10 fast high-knees in front of the right safety mat (J).
- Afterwards, 2 does 10 push-ups on the safety mat (10 sit-ups in the next round).
- 2 passes his handball to the coach and the course starts over (K).

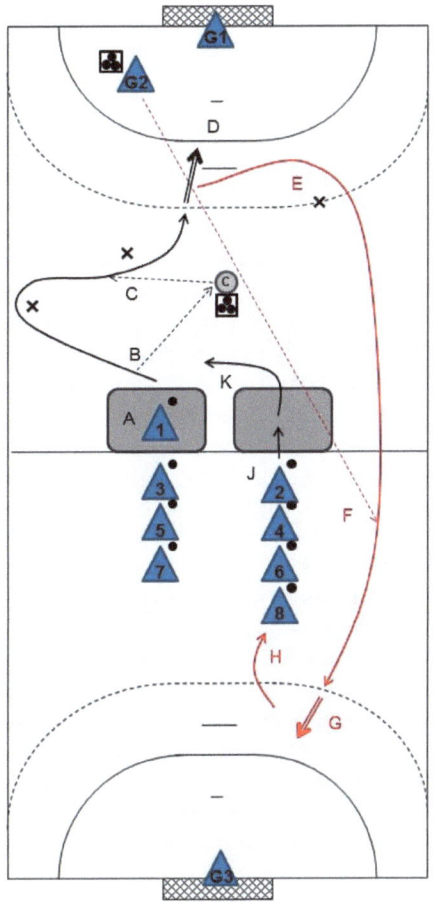

⚠ Exchange the goalkeepers after a while.

⚠ The players must time their start in such a way that the goalkeepers have sufficient time for their actions.

Varied handball shooting drills
60 exercises for every handball training unit

No. 16	Series of shots at defined corners	7	★★
Equipment required:	2 small gym mats, 4 cards in different colors, 2 ball boxes with sufficient number of handballs		

Setting:
- Position the mats as shown in the figure.

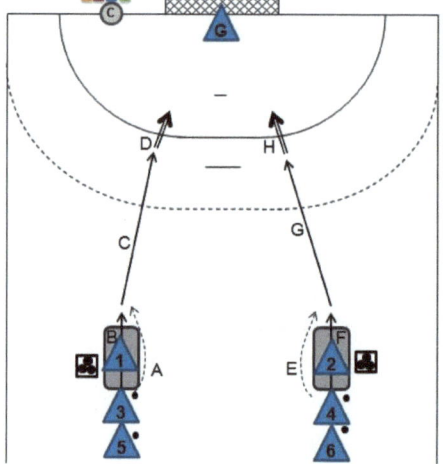

Course 1:
- ▲1 and ▲2 stand on the mat with their feet shoulder-width apart.
- ▲3 throws his handball over ▲1 (A), crawls through the legs of ▲1, and catches his handball (B).
- Afterwards, ▲3 dribbles towards the goal (C) and shoots (D).
- While the player approaches the goal (C), the coach shows one of

the colored cards, which indicates the goal corner at which ▲3 must shoot (e.g., green: bottom right, blue: top right, red: bottom left, orange: top left).
- While ▲3 is shooting (D), ▲4 starts the same drill on the other side (E-H), etc.

Variant on the mat:
- ▲1 and ▲2 stand on the mat and bend forward with their arms resting on their knees.
- ▲3 throws his handball over ▲1 (A), jumps over ▲1, and catches his handball. (B) → leap.

⚠ The players should catch their handball in the air immediately after the crawling/leaping, if possible.

⚠ Even if they made a mistake in the previous exercise, the players should nevertheless secure their ball quickly and shoot at the goal (according to the card shown).

⚠ Substitute ▲1 and ▲2 regularly.

| No. 17 | Series of shots with previous reaction exercise | 7 | ★★ |

Equipment required: 3 small vaulting boxes, 7 cones (different colors), 1 handball per player

Setting:
- Position three small vaulting boxes with one cone in front of each box and two cones of different colors on the left and right side each (see figure).

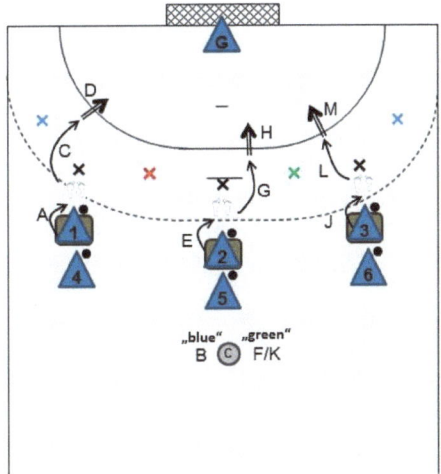

Course 1:
- 1 jumps from the vaulting box with both legs while holding his handball (A).
- While he jumps, the coach calls out the color of one of the neighboring cones (here "blue" – B).
- 1 approaches the goal on the side of the respective cone (C) without dribbling (and within the 3-step rule) and shoots (D).
- Afterwards, 2 jumps from the vaulting box with both legs (E) and the coach calls out a color again (here "green" – F).
- 2 approaches the goal on the respective side (G) and shoots (H).
- Afterwards, 3 jumps from the vaulting box with both legs (J); the coach calls out a color once again (here "green" again – K).
- 3 approaches the goal on the respective side (L) and shoots (M).
- Start the course over with 4, 5, and 6.

Course 2:
- As in course 1, the coach calls out a color first and thus determines the side on which the player must approach the goal. However, he also calls out "2" or "3" and thus determines how many steps the player may take before shooting at the goal (e.g., "blue 2": two steps, on the side of the blue cone; "red 3": three steps, on the side of the red cone).

⚠️ The players should react immediately, approach the goal as instructed, and shoot. They have to shoot in a highly concentrated manner however.

No. 18	Series of shots with two variants and decision-making	10	★★
Equipment required:	2 small gym mats, 4 poles, 2 ball boxes with sufficient number of handballs		

Setting:
- Position two small gym mats and poles as shown in the figure.

Course:
- 1 starts and does 10 jumping jacks on the mat while holding his handball (A).
- Afterwards, 1 makes a piston movement (B) and passes the ball to the coach (C).
- 1 dynamically moves to the outside and runs a curve around the pole (D).
- Once he has run around the pole, 1 receives a pass into his running path (E) and shoots at the goal at full speed (F).
- 2 starts the same drill on the other side (delayed) (G-M).

Course 2:
- 1 starts and does 8 straight jumps on the mat with both legs while holding his handball (A).
- Afterwards, 1 makes a piston movement (B), passes the ball to the coach (C), dynamically moves towards the outside, runs a curve around the pole (D), and receives a return pass from the coach (E).
- 1 passes the ball to the wing position to 3 (F) who runs a curve and eventually shoots at the goal (G).
- 2 starts the same course on the other side (delayed) (H-N).
- After he has played the pass, 1 lines up on the wing position. 3 picks up a ball and lines up behind 2.

Course 3:

- The drill remains the same as in course 2; however, add a defense player on each side.
- Once ① has received the pass from the coach (E), he must decide:
    - If ① plays defensively, ① shoots over the block (F).
    - If ① steps forward, the ball must be passed to the player on the wing position who eventually shoots at the goal (G).

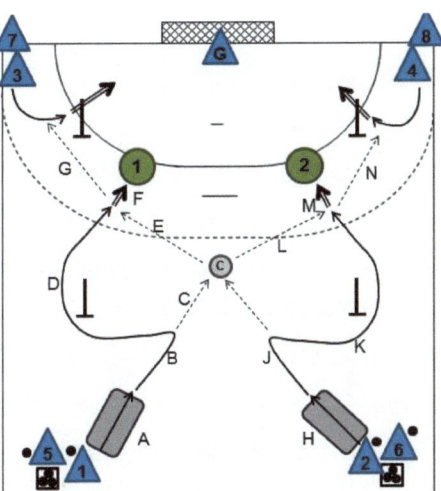

No. 19	Series of shots with coordination and passing	7	★★
Equipment required:	6 cones, ball box with sufficient number of handballs		

Setting:
- Use two cones to define each running path (it should form an "8").
- Put two more cones on the floor to define the running path for the subsequent action (see figure).

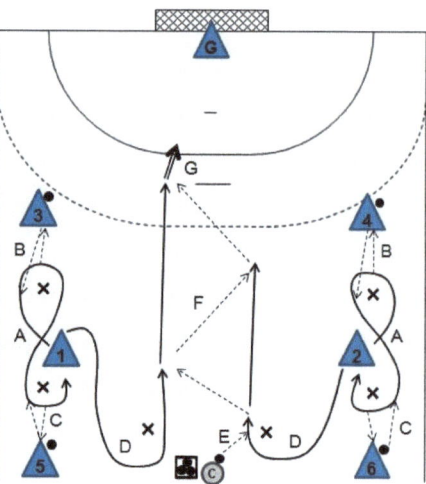

Course:
- **1** and **2** start simultaneously; their running path around the two cones should form an "8" (A).
- While running, they alternately play double passes (B and C) with the receivers (**3** and **5**, **4** and **6**, respectively).
- When the coach whistles, **1** and **2** run around the cones in the back without a ball (D).
- The coach passes a ball to one of the two players (E). **1** and **2** keep running towards the goal and passing to each other (F) until one of them is in shooting position (G).
- As soon as the coach has whistled, one receiver each starts running the "8 path". A new player becomes the second receiver and the course starts over.

⚠ The players should run the "8 path" smoothly (A). Also, they should not interrupt their running moves when they play and receive a pass.

⚠ On command, the players should run around the cones and pass the ball as fast as possible (D) until one of them shoots at the goal (E, F, and G).

Varied handball shooting drills
60 exercises for every handball training unit

No. 20	Series of shots with defensive block and fast break	9	★★
Equipment required:	1 small vaulting box, 5 cones, 2 ball boxes with sufficient number of handballs		

Setting:
- Position a small vaulting box and three cones as shown in the figure.

Course:
- 1 starts and quickly jumps up and down the vaulting box five times with both legs (A).
- After he has jumped five times, 1 immediately sprints towards the second cone, backwards to the first cone (B), forwards to the third cone (while passing the ball to 2 (C)), and backwards to the second cone. Afterwards, 1 approaches the goal dynamically and receives a pass from 2 into his running path (D).
- 1 makes a jump shot over 1 who serves as defensive block (E).
- Once he has shot, 1 immediately starts to run a fast break (F), receives a pass from 5 into his running path (G), and eventually shoots at the goal (H).
- Once 1 has received the return pass from 2 (D), 3 starts jumping up and down the small vaulting box (A), etc.
- The passing players (2 and 5) and the defensive player (1) are substituted with other players after a few passes, etc.
- Repeat the drill until each player has done 5 to 10 rounds (shots and fast breaks).

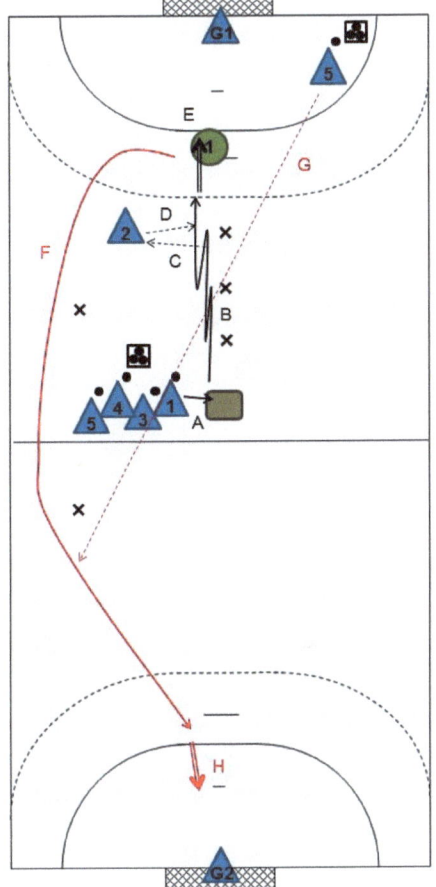

⚠ The drill should be done dynamically. The players must switch immediately after the jump shot (E) and run a fast break (at top speed).

Varied handball shooting drills
60 exercises for every handball training unit

No. 21	Series of shots with penalties	6	★★
Equipment required:	1 small gym mat, 2 cones, 1 ball box with sufficient number of handballs			

Setting:
- Put cones and mats on the floor as shown in the figure.

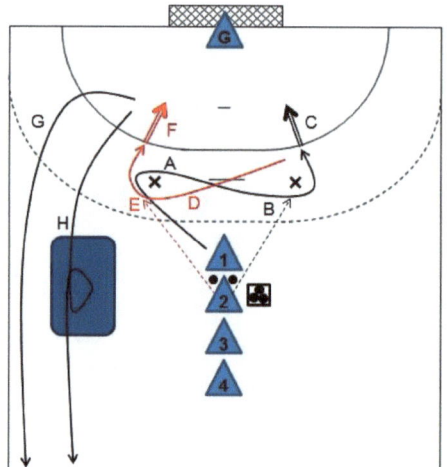

Course:
- 1 starts without a ball, runs a slalom around both cones (A), and receives a pass from 2 into his running path (B).
- 1 runs around the second cone, approaches the goal dynamically, and shoots eventually (C).
- After he has shot, 1 immediately starts the next action, runs around the cone (D), receives a second pass from 2 (E), and eventually shoots at the goal (F).
    - If 1 hit the goal twice, he sprints a curve towards the center line (G).
    - If he missed the goal once, 1 sprints towards the small gym mat and does a forward somersault (H) before sprinting towards the center line (J).
    - If he missed the goal twice, 1 sprints to the small gym mat and does a forward and a backward somersault (H) before sprinting towards the center line (J).
- 1 lines up again and the drill starts over with 2, etc.
- Change sides after a while.

⚠ Following each action, the players should start the consecutive action dynamically.

Varied handball shooting drills
60 exercises for every handball training unit

No. 22	Series of shots with previous coordination exercise and consecutive action	9	★★★
Equipment required:	8 hoops, 2 cones, ball box with sufficient number of handballs		

Setting:
- Position hoops and cones as shown in the figure.

Course:
- 1 and 2 (with a ball) start simultaneously and jump through the line of hoops with both legs (A).
- After the line of hoops, they speed up considerably and make an extensive body feint in front of the cone (B).
- 2 dribbles towards the center and crosses 1 who runs towards him dynamically (C).
- 1 makes a jump shot (D).
- After the pass (C), 2 immediately runs around the cone (E), receives a pass from 7 into his running path (F), and makes a jump shot (G).
- After he has shot, 1 fetches a new ball and lines up behind 8. 2 lines up behind 5 without a ball. 7 fetches a new ball and lines up behind 6.

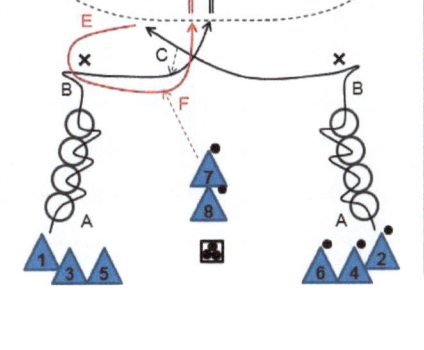

Variants:
- Jump with one leg (left/right).
- Add a defense player who acts defensively on the 6-meter line.

⚠ The players should jump through the line of hoops quickly but properly.

⚠ Dynamic running movements

⚠ After the crossing, the player (2) must adjust to the new situation immediately and start the second action (E).

No. 23	Shooting during endurance training	8	★★★
Equipment required:	8 cones, 2 ball boxes with sufficient number of handballs		

Setting:
- Position cones as shown in the figure.

Course:
- The players run around the square of cones in the center of the court at moderate pace (A).
- On command, ① starts a series of three shots (the other players keep running around the cones at moderate pace).
- ① may choose the position from which he wants to shoot at the goal (LW, LB, CB, RB, RW).
- ① receives a pass from the feeder into his running path (B and C) and shoots at the goal (D).
- Once he has shot, ① sprints around the cone (E) and receives another pass from the feeder into his running path.
- After the third shot, ① runs to the opposite goal at increasing speed (F). Once he has arrived, he does three 7-meter penalty shots (G).
- Additional task after six shots: The number of missed shots divided by 2 (round up, if applicable) will be the number of rounds which ① must sprint around the square of cones in the center of the court afterwards (A). Three missed shots = sprint 2 rounds (A).
- After he has sprinted his rounds, ① keeps running at moderate pace until it is his turn again.
- Following the first three shots of ① , it is the next player's turn.

Repetition:
- Each player does the drill twice (2 × 6 shots).
- Afterwards, the players may take a short break before the drill starts over; however, now the 1:1-rule applies. Each missed shot will be one "penalty round". However, if they score three times at the 7-meter line, the players nullify any missed attempts they have made during their first three shots and, hence, do not have to sprint.

No. 24	Series of shots with athletics drill	11	★★★
Equipment required:	6 hurdles, 1 handball per player		

Setting:
- Position the hurdles (or small vaulting boxes) as shown in the figure.
- Divide the team into three groups:
    - Two shooting exercise groups (1, 2, 3, and 4, 5, 6)
    - One strengthening exercise group (7, 8, and 9)

Course:
- 1 passes his handball to C (A) and jumps over both hurdles (with both legs at the same time) without making an intermediate hop between the hurdles (the players may touch the floor between the hurdles one time only).
- 4 starts the same course in parallel with 1 (J).
- While jumping over the second hurdle, 1 receives a return pass from C shortly before he touches the ground again (C). 1 must land with both feet.

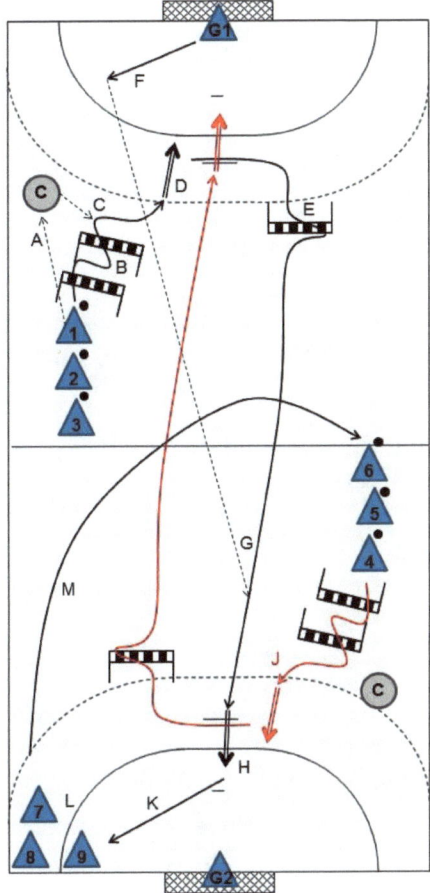

- Now, 1 starts to run towards the goal, without dribbling however (i.e. observing the 3-step rule), and eventually makes a jump shot (D).
- After the shot, 1 jumps over the hurdle with both legs (E), dynamically starts to run a fast break, receives a long pass from the goalkeeper G1 (G), and eventually shoots at the opposite goal (H).
- The goalkeeper's G1 position should allow him to play the long pass in an optimal way (i.e. diagonally) (F).
- After he has shot, 1 joins the strengthening exercise group (L) on the side

(K) and does 10 push-ups and 10 sit-ups alternately. **7** gets up and joins the 1st shooting exercise group (M).
- After he has shot, **4** lines up again behind **3**.
- Repeat until each player has been in each group 10 to 15 times.

⚠ Adjust hurdle height to the players' level of performance, i.e. in such a way that the players can jump over the hurdles with both legs at the same time.

⚠ Both shooting exercise groups have to start simultaneously in order to give the goalkeepers enough time to position themselves correctly after they have thrown the long pass for the fast break.

⚠ During the exercise, all players have to be highly concentrated in order to prevent collisions on the running paths.

Category: Shooting training for specific playing positions

No. 25	Shooting from individual positions 1	3	★
Equipment required:	2 cones, 1 handball per player		

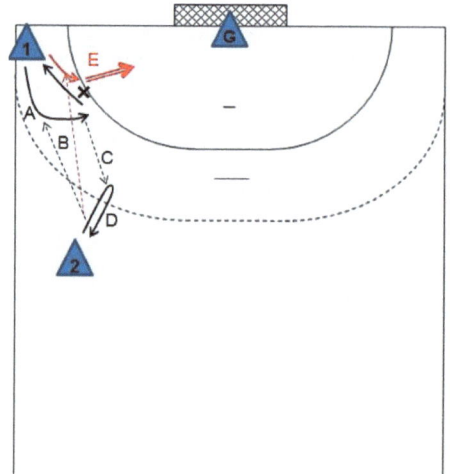

Setting:
- 1 to 2 players stand on each position (LW, LB, CB, RB, RW). The drill is done on one position after the other.

Course on the LW (RW) position:
- **1** runs a curve (A) and receives a pass from **2** (B). **1** makes a dynamic piston movement towards the side of the cone and plays a return pass to **2** who also does the piston movement (C).
- Following the action, **1** and **2** immediately move back to their initial positions (D).
- Repeat the course a second time.
- After the third course, **1** makes a piston movement towards the outer side, receives a bounce pass from **2** into his running path, and eventually shoots at the goal (E).

Varied handball shooting drills
60 exercises for every handball training unit

Course on the LB (RB) position:

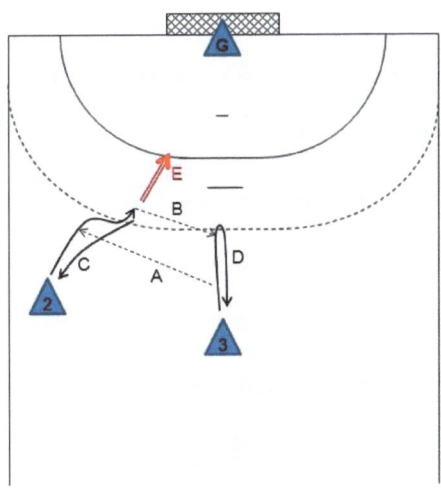

- 2 dynamically runs a curve and makes a piston movement while receiving the pass from 3 into his running path (A).
- Afterwards, he plays a return pass to 3 (B) who also does the piston movement.
- Following their action, 2 and 3 both move back to their initial positions immediately (C and D) and repeat the course.
- After the third course, 3 does not receive a return pass, but 2 makes a jump shot at the goal (E).

Course on the CB position:

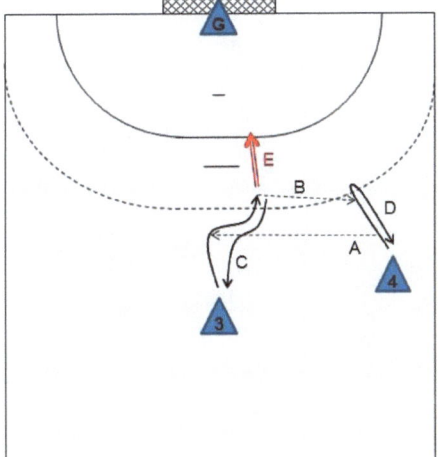

- 3 dynamically runs a curve and makes a piston movement while receiving the pass from 4 into his running path (A).
- Afterwards, he plays a return pass to 4 (B) who also does the piston movement.
- Following their action, 3 and 4 both immediately move back to their initial positions (C and D) and repeat the course.
- After the third course, 4 does not receive a return pass, but 3 makes a jump shot at the goal (E).
- Afterwards, the players do the same course as on the left side on the RB and RW positions.

⚠ The players may not take a break between the courses. Once the players on the LW position have shot, the course immediately starts on the RB position, etc.

⚠ Make sure the players do the piston movement dynamically.

Varied handball shooting drills
60 exercises for every handball training unit

No. 26	Shooting from positions with coordination run	3	★
Equipment required:	3 cones, ball box with sufficient number of handballs		

Setting:
- Define the running paths with cones (see figures).

Course on the wing positions:
- 1 runs an "8 path" around the cones, receives a pass from 2 into his running path (A), and shoots from the wing position (B).
- Afterwards, 1 immediately starts running the "8 path" and the course starts over (C).

Repetitions:
- 10 shots in a competition with a second/third wing player. Who has scored most often after 10 shots?

Course on the back positions:
- 1 runs an "8 path" around the cones. Afterwards, he receives a pass from 2 into his running path (A) and shoots from the back position at full speed (B).
- Afterwards, 1 immediately starts running the "8 path" and the course starts over (C).

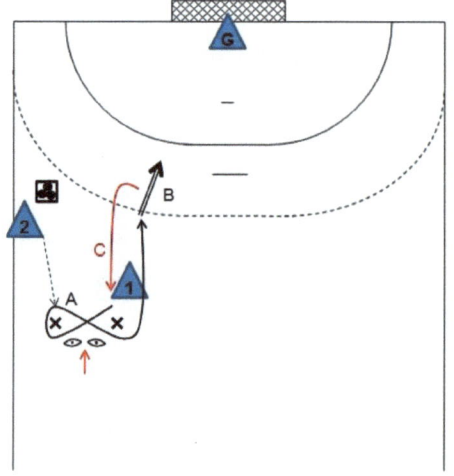

Repetitions:
- 10 shots in competition with a second/third back position player. Who has scored most often after 10 shots?

⚠ While running the "8 path", the players must always face the goal.

No. 27	Series of shots for the wing players with previous exertion	8	★

Equipment required: 4 cones, ball box with sufficient number of handballs

Course:

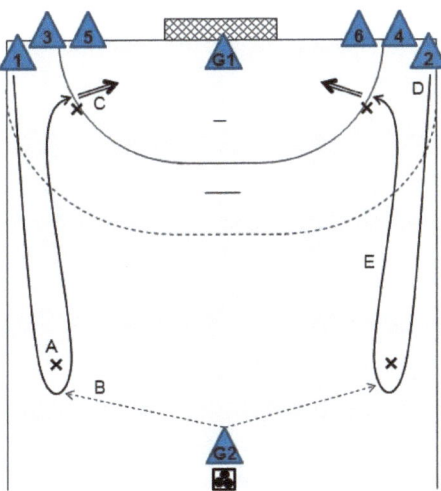

- ① sprints around the cone (A) and receives a pass into his running path (B).
- ① sprints back (dribbling) and shoots at the goal from the wing position (C).
- Immediately before ① shoots at the goal (C), ② starts the same course on the other side (D).
- Once ① has shot and ② approaches the goal (E), ① starts the course over.
- Each player does the course three times, alternating with the players on the other side. Afterwards, it is the next two players' turn (③ and ④).

⚠ The players should do three actions in a row at top speed.

⚠ However, they must time their actions in such a way that the goalkeeper has sufficient time to move from one side to the other and position himself correctly for the shot from the opposite wing position. The players may start slightly delayed!

No. 28	Series of shots for the back position players	3	★
Equipment required:	5 cones, sufficient number of handballs		

Setting:
- Array five cones as shown in the figure.

Course:
- 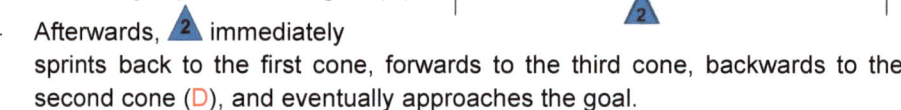 2 starts from the center line, sprints towards the second cone, runs backwards to the first cone, and eventually approaches the goal (A).
- 1 passes the ball into the running path of 2 (B) and 2 makes a jump shot at the goal (C).
- Afterwards, 2 immediately sprints back to the first cone, forwards to the third cone, backwards to the second cone (D), and eventually approaches the goal.
- 1 passes the ball into the running path of 2 (E) and 2 makes a jump shot at the goal (F).

Repeat the course for the other cones as follows:
- Sprint back to the second cone, towards the fourth cone, backwards to the third cone, and eventually approach the goal.
- Sprint back to the third cone, towards the fifth cone, backwards to the fourth cone, and eventually approach the goal.

Afterwards, another player starts the course over. Subsequently, 2 repeats the course once more (each player has to do the course twice with a short break in between).

⚠ Make sure the players do the course in a highly dynamic manner.

Varied handball shooting drills
60 exercises for every handball training unit

No. 29	Series of shots for the CB player	6	★
Equipment required:	1 cone, ball box with sufficient number of handballs		

Course:

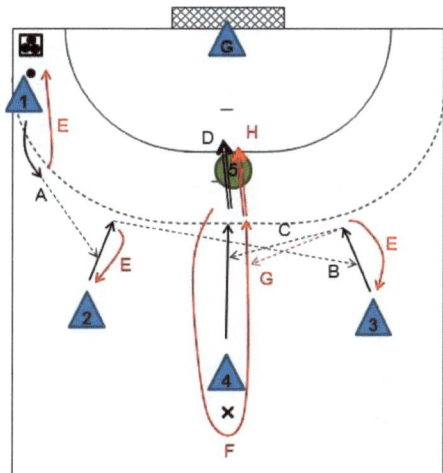

- 1 runs a curve, makes a piston movement, and passes the ball into the running path of 2 (A).
- 2 makes a piston movement and passes the ball into the running path of 3 (B).
- 3 makes a piston movement and passes the ball into the running path of 4 (C).
- 4 makes a jump shot at the goal (D). 5 serves as defensive block.
- Following their actions, 1, 2, and 3 immediately move back to their initial positions (E) and start the course over (A and B).
- Immediately after he has shot (D), 4 sprints around the cone (F), receives a second pass into his running path (G), and makes a jump shot at the goal (H).
- After the second shot of 4, 5 and 4 switch tasks and the course starts over.

Repetitions:

- 4 and 5 each do four series of shots (8 shots each). Afterwards, the five players switch positions (e.g., clockwise).

⚠ Position the cone (behind 4) in such a way that 3 does not have to wait before he passes the ball to 4 (1 times the initial pass).

⚠ 2 and 3 make a complete piston movement and move back immediately after they have played the pass.

⚠ The drill is to be done in a highly dynamic manner.

No. 30	Series of shots for the pivot	5	★
Equipment required:	Ball box with sufficient number of handballs		

Setting:

- ① and ② stand next to each other at the 6-meter line.
- They lift their arms at an angle of 90° so that their fingertips touch and their arms form a "tunnel".

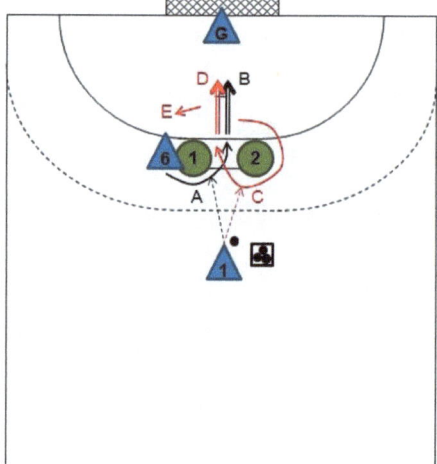

Course:

- ⑥ starts from the left side of ①, runs around him, and receives a pass from ① into his running path (A).
- ⑥ dynamically runs through the "arm tunnel" of ① and ② and shoots from the 6-meter line (B).
- Once he has shot, ⑥ immediately runs around ②, receives a pass from ① into his running path (C), dynamically runs through the "arm tunnel" of ① and ②, and shoots from the 6-meter line again (D).
- Afterwards, the course starts over, ⑥ runs around ① (E), etc.

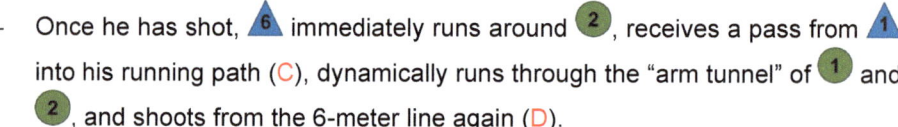

⚠ ⑥ should duck while running through the "arm tunnel" of ① and ②, then immediately straighten up dynamically, and eventually shoot at the goal.

Varied handball shooting drills
60 exercises for every handball training unit

No. 31	Series of shots for the wing players 2	6	★★
Equipment required:	1 cone, ball box with sufficient number of handballs		

Setting:
- Define the shooting position with a cone.

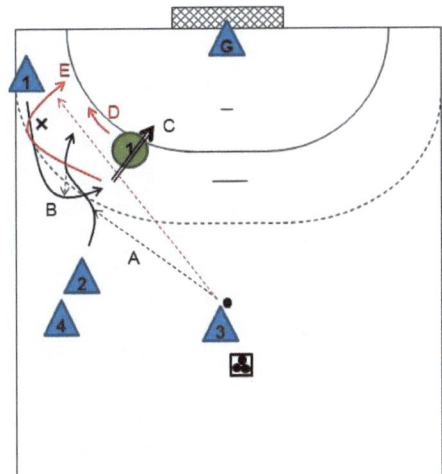

Course:
- ③ passes the ball into the running path of ② (A).
- ② makes a dynamic piston movement and crosses ① who runs a curve coming from the wing position (B).
- ① makes a jump shot (C) over ①.
- Following the defense action, ① immediately moves to the wing position (D) in order to interfere with the subsequent shot of ①.
- Once he has shot, ① immediately moves back, runs around the cone, receives a pass from ③ into his running path, and shoots from the wing position (E).
- ① repeats the course 5 times without a break. Afterwards, the tasks are reallocated.

⚠️ ① serves as defensive block. He should interfere (sometimes more, sometimes less) with the shot of ① from the wing position, but allow the shot in the end.

⚠️ ① must do 10 actions in total in a highly dynamic manner.

Varied handball shooting drills
60 exercises for every handball training unit

No. 32	Series of shots for the LB and RB players with exertion	9	★★
Equipment required:	6 cones, ball box with sufficient number of handballs		

Setting:
- Array two lines of cones as shown in the figure.

Course:

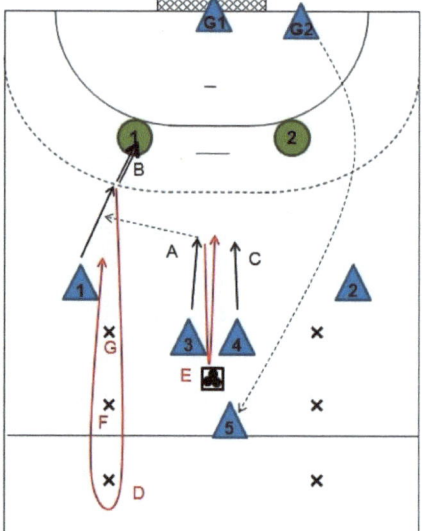

- 3 makes a piston movement and passes the ball into the running path of 1 (A).
- 1 makes a jump shot over 1 who serves as defensive block (B).
- 4 makes a piston movement (C) and passes the ball into the running path of 2 who also makes a jump shot at the goal.
- After the shot, 1 sprints around the backmost cone (D).
- 3 fetches a new ball (E) and once again passes it into the running path of 1 who makes a jump shot at the goal.
- Afterwards, it is the turn of 2 again.
- 1 and 2 then sprint around the center cone (F) and eventually around the foremost cone (G).
- G2 passes the balls that have been shot at the goal to 5 who stands at the center line and puts them back into the ball box.

⚠️ 1 and 2 must time their shots in such a way that the goalkeeper has sufficient time to position himself correctly between the shots.

⚠️ 1 and 2 should sprint around the cones (D, F, and G).

Varied handball shooting drills
60 exercises for every handball training unit

No. 33	Series of shots for the back positions and running moves without the ball	8	★★
Equipment required:	12 cones, ball box with sufficient number of handballs		

Setting:
- Define two corridors using cones (see figure).

Course:
- 1 steps forward and does five quick jumping jacks on the spot (A).
- Afterwards, 1 runs a curve to the right side and through the corridor of cones (B).
- 1 rotates his body backwards and receives a pass from 2 into his running path from behind (C).
- 1 makes a jump shot over 3 who serves as defensive block (D). After the shot, 1 becomes the new defense player (E).
- Following the defense action, 3 fetches a new ball and lines up (F).
- Immediately after the pass, 2 starts doing the jumping jacks (G) and the course starts over on the other side.
- And so on.

Variants:
- The players do push-ups, sit-ups, or straight jumps as their initial action (A).

⚠️ After the initial action (A), 1 should start to run as dynamically as possible (B).

No. 34	Series of shots for the pivot 2	6	★★
Equipment required:	Ball box with sufficient number of handballs		

Basic course:
- The pivot (2) does eight actions in a row (four actions on each side). Switch tasks afterwards (new pivot, defense player, feeder).

Course 1:
- The defense players 2 and 3 stand face-to-face holding hands.
- 2 starts from the left side, runs around 2 (A), receives a pass from 1 into his running path (B), jumps through the gap between 2 and 3, and shoots (C).
- 2 breaks through the barrier (i.e. the arms of 2 and 3). The two defense players hold hands loosely so that they can let go at the time of the break-through. However, they do not let go before 2 has touched them.
- Afterwards, 2 turns around, holds hands with 1, and 2 starts for the next shot from the other side.

Course 2:
- The defense players leave a larger gap than in course 1 and do not hold hands anymore.
- 2 starts from the left side, runs around 2 (A), receives a pass from 1 into his running path (B), and tries to jump through the gap between 2 and 3 (C).
- If 2 moves towards 3 and closes the gap on this side, (D), 2 moves around 2 and shoots on the left side of 2 (E).

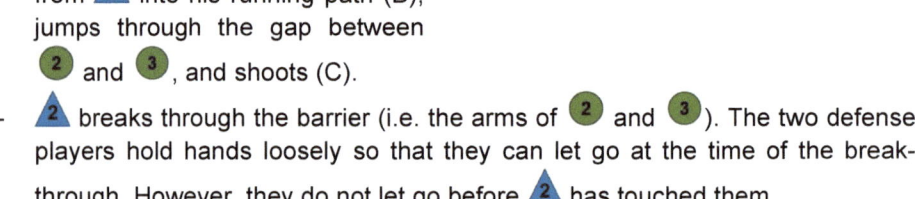

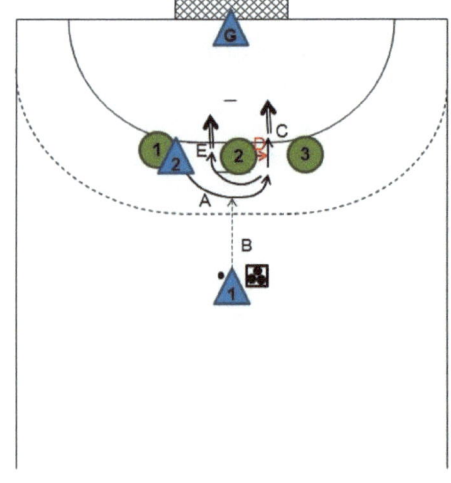

- 2 starts the next round on the right side.

⚠ The outer defense players hold their positions; only 2 may close the gap.

⚠ 2 should move dynamically at the 6-meter line and jump through the gaps courageously.

No. 35	Series of shots from the back positions with block	6	★★
Equipment required:	2 cones, ball box with sufficient number of handballs		

Basic course:
- The players who are currently not involved in the drill pick up the handballs so that the shooting players do not have to wait.
- Two players each shoot three times alternately (9 shots per player in total).

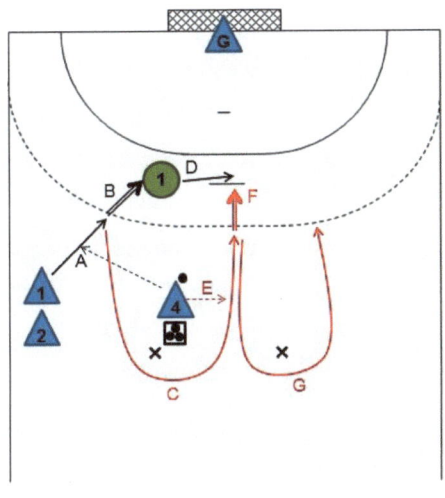

Course:
- 1 approaches the goal dynamically, receives a pass from 4 into his running path (A), and makes a jumps shot over 1 who serves as defensive block (B).
- Once he has shot, 1 runs around the cone immediately (C).
- 1 moves towards the next shooting position (D).
- 1 receives the next pass from 4 into his running path (E) and makes a jump shot, again over the defensive block of 1 (F).
- Repeat the course a third time on the RB position (G).
- Following the third shot, the course starts over with 2.
- And so on.

⚠ 1 and G should keep communicating regarding the defensive block (defense corner/goalkeeper corner).

No. 36	Series of shots with decision-making on the back and wing positions	7	★★
Equipment required:	3 cones, ball box with sufficient number of handballs		

Setting:
- Position cones as shown in the figure.

Course on the back positions:

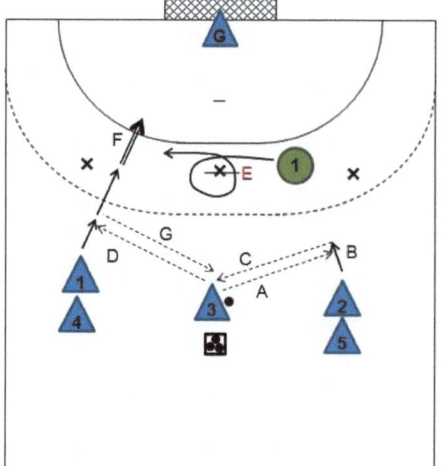

- ③ starts the drill and passes a ball into the running path of one of the back position players (here ②) (A and B).
- If ① stands in the way of ②, ② passes the ball back to ③ (C), and ③ passes the ball to ① (D).
- ① runs around the cone in the center and then tries to position himself in the way of ① (E):
  - If ① has not managed to get into a proper position in time, ① makes a jump shot (F).
  - If ① is already in position, ① passes the ball back to ③ (G) and the players repeat the drill on the other side.
- After they have shot, the shooters line up again. ③ passes a new ball immediately.

⚠ The players should observe ① and decide whether to shoot or to play a return pass once they have received the ball.

Course on the wing positions:

- **1** makes a slight piston movement towards the center while holding the ball (A) and passes it to **2** (B).
- While **1** plays the pass to **2** (B), **1** starts and runs around the cone (C).
- After he has passed the ball, **1** moves back in order to initiate a piston movement towards the outer side again (E).
- **2** makes a piston movement (D) and passes the ball into the running path of **1** (F).
- **1** approaches the goal and shoots (G).
- If **1** has already run around the cones and stands between **1** and the goal, **1** may pass the ball to **2** one more time and the players repeat the drill (C-G).
- After the shot, the drill starts over on the other side (H and J).
- Each wing player shoots five times in a row (alternating with the players on the other side).

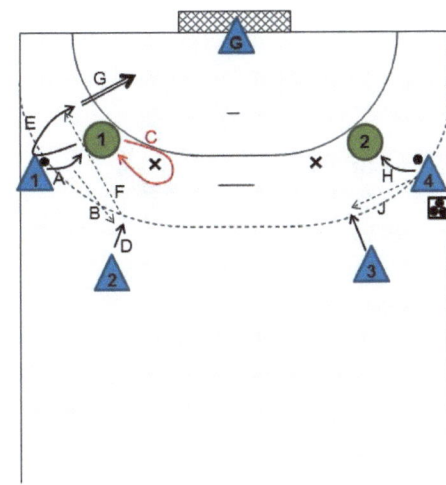

⚠️ **1** should decide whether shooting (G) is possible. He should approach the goal dynamically and also try to break through smaller spaces on the wing position.

Varied handball shooting drills
60 exercises for every handball training unit

No. 37	Shooting circle training for specific playing positions	8	★★
Equipment required:	2 large vaulting boxes, 2 small vaulting boxes, 2 small gym mats, 6 cones, 3 tennis balls, 1 handball per player		

Course on the wing positions:
- Position a large vaulting box on each side as shown in the figure.
- ▲1 (▲3 on the right side) starts from the wing position, throws his ball at the large vaulting box (A), starts to run, picks up the ball bouncing back, and shoots at the goal (B).

Course on the pivot position:
- Position two small vaulting boxes as shown in the figure, with the upholstered side facing inside.
- ▲2 throws his ball at the small vaulting box (C), runs around the cone, picks up the ball again, and shoots at the goal (D).

Course on the small gym mats:
- The players on the small gym mats do sit-ups (E).

Course on the back positions:
- ▲4 throws the ball in the air (forwards) (F), runs a slalom around the cones as shown in the figure (G), picks up the ball again, and makes a jump shot at the goal within the three-step rule (without dribbling) (H).

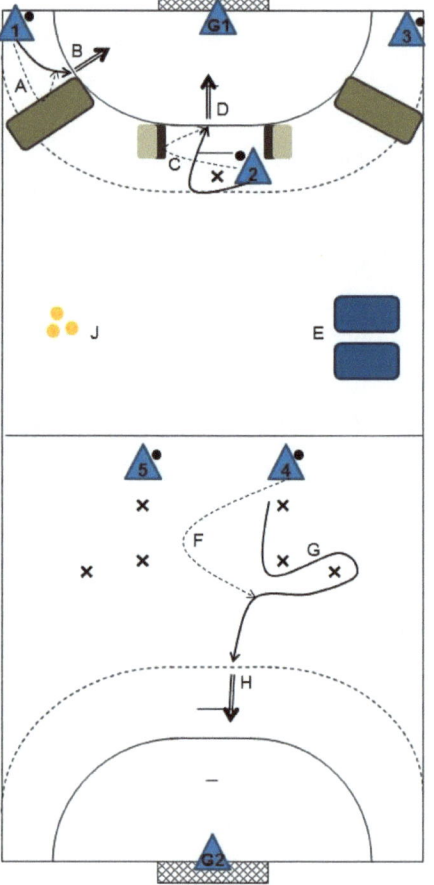

Course for the tennis balls:
- The players should juggle with three tennis balls (J).

Basic course:
- The players do the individual exercises in rotation (e.g., three shots from a position, then move on to the next position) so that each player has done the predefined number of exercises on each position:

- 3 rounds in total:
  - 9 shots from each position = 45 shots
  - 3 × 20 sit-ups
  - 3 × 1 to 2 minutes of juggling

⚠ The drill can also be done with one goalkeeper and 3 to 4 field players. The players do each exercise simultaneously and in rotation.

No. 38	Series of shots for the back positions with crossing 1	10	★★
Equipment required:	Sufficient number of handballs		

Setting:
- One player stands on the left and one on the right wing position.
- A minimum of two players stand on each back position.

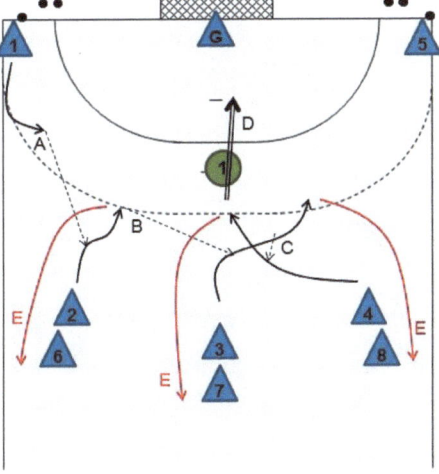

Course:
- 1️⃣ dynamically runs a curve coming from the wing position, makes a piston movement while holding the ball, and passes it into the running path of 2️⃣ (A).
- 2️⃣ makes a dynamic piston movement and passes the ball into the running path of 3️⃣ (B).
- 3️⃣ crosses 4️⃣ dynamically (C).
- 4️⃣ makes a jump shot (D) (🟢 serves as defensive block and tries to block the shot).
- Following their action, the players (2️⃣, 3️⃣, and 4️⃣) move back immediately as shown in the figure (E).
- After 4️⃣ has shot (D), the players repeat the course on the other side.
- And so on.

⚠ 🟢 might have to adjust his position to the left or to the right side.

⚠ Make sure that the players do the drill dynamically.

No. 39	Series of shots for the back positions with crossing 2	7	★★
Equipment required:	1 cone, ball box with sufficient number of handballs		

Setting:
- Define the running path with a cone.

Course:

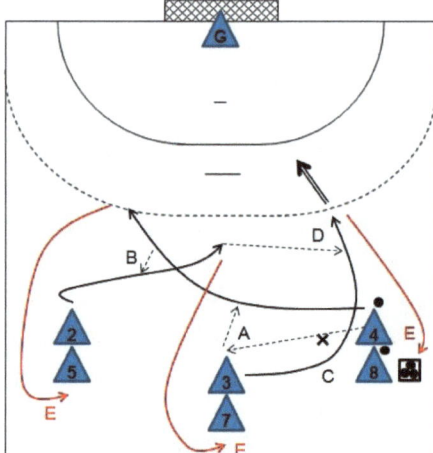

- ▲4 passes the ball to ▲3, dynamically runs to the left side, and receives a return pass from ▲3 into his running path (A).
- ▲2 makes a running feint to the left side (without a ball) and crosses ▲4 who passes the ball (B).
- After ▲3 has played the pass to ▲4 (A), he runs around the cone (C).
- ▲2 now approaches the goal with the ball and passes it to ▲3 who runs towards him at full speed (D).
- ▲3 makes a jump shot at the 9-meter line.
- After the action, the players line up again as shown in the figure (E), etc.

⚠ ▲3 must time his start in such a way that he does not have to wait for the pass (D).

No. 40	Series of shots for the wing players with crossing on the back positions	8	★★
Equipment required:	Ball box with sufficient number of handballs		

Course:

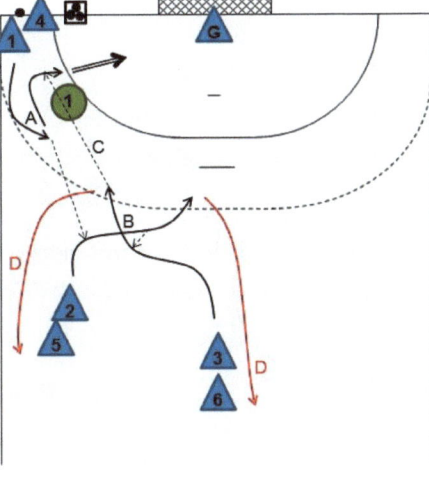

- ① dynamically runs a curve coming from the wing position, makes a piston movement while holding the ball, and passes it to ② (A). Afterwards, ① moves back to the corner immediately.
- ② starts a dynamic piston movement and crosses ③ (B).
- ③ approaches the goal and plays a bounce pass to ① (C) who shoots from the wing position.
- Immediately after the shot, ④ starts the same course.
- And so on.
- After the action, ② and ③ move back immediately and line up again (D).

⚠ ① acts defensively in the beginning, but tries to interfere with the shooter more and more offensively during the course. He should allow the shot however.

Category: Complex series of shots

No. 41	Series of shots with previous exercise	3	★★
Equipment required:	2 coordination ladders, 2 cones, ball box with sufficient number of handballs		

Setting:
- Put two coordination ladders on the floor and align them in parallel. Position two cones, one on the left and one on the right, as shown in the figure.
- The coach stands at the side next to the ball box that contains additional handballs.

Course:
- 1 and 2 sidestep (face-to-face) through the coordination ladder (two footsteps per interspace) (A) while passing the ball (B and C).
- At the end of the coordination ladder, the players change the direction and sidestep to the other side.
- On the coach's command ("GO"), the player holding the ball (here 2) runs towards the goal (D) and shoots (E).
- The other player (1) runs around one of the two cones (F).
- The coach rolls another ball into the court (G), 1 picks it up (H), runs towards the goal, and shoots (J).
- On the coach's command "GO" for 1 and 2, the next two players start to pass and sidestep through the coordination ladder immediately.

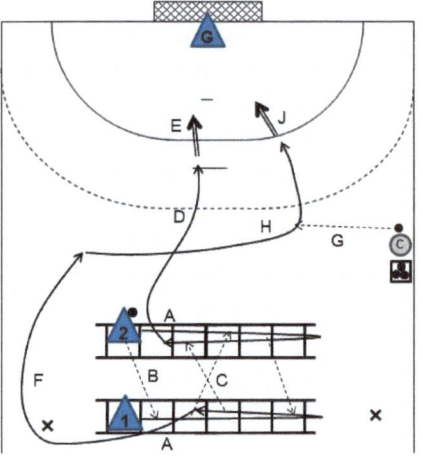

⚠ The players should react immediately on the coach's command and start the respective subsequent action.

Varied handball shooting drills
60 exercises for every handball training unit

No. 42	Initial actions as series of shots from different positions	10	★★

Equipment required: Ball box with sufficient number of handballs

Setting:
- A minimum of two players stand on each position. One player on the CB position is sufficient however.

Course 1:

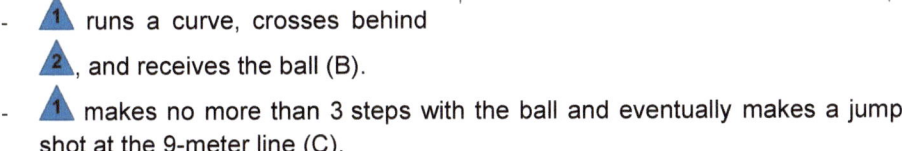

- 3 starts a piston movement and passes the ball to 2 (A). Afterwards, he moves back to his initial position.
- 2 makes a dynamic piston movement towards the goal.
- 1 runs a curve, crosses behind 2, and receives the ball (B).
- 1 makes no more than 3 steps with the ball and eventually makes a jump shot at the 9-meter line (C).
- Afterwards, 1 and 2 switch positions.
- 3 starts the piston movement again and passes the ball to 4 (D). Repeat the course on the other side.

Variant:
- Position a block for the shooting wing player (1).

⚠ Substitute the feeder on the CB position after a few passes.

Course 2:

- 3 starts a piston movement and passes the ball to 2 (A). Afterwards, he moves back to his initial position.
- 2 makes a dynamic piston movement towards the goal.
- 1 runs a curve, crosses behind 2, and receives the ball (B).
- 1 runs towards the 7-meter line while holding the ball and passes it into the running path of 4 (C) who approaches the goal dynamically.

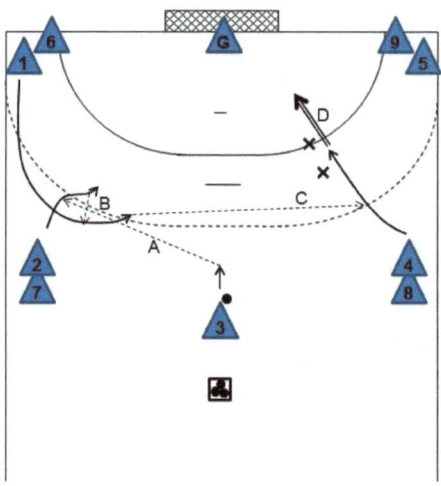

- 4 runs towards the goal and shoots at full speed from 6 to 7 meters (D).
- Afterwards, 1 and 2 switch positions.
- 3 starts the piston movement again and passes the ball to 8. Repeat the course on the other side.

⚠ 1 must play a straight and fast pass to 4 (no banana pass).

Course 3:

- 3 starts a piston movement and passes the ball to 2 (A). Afterwards, he moves back to his initial position.
- 2 makes a dynamic piston movement towards the goal.
- 1 runs a curve, crosses behind 2, and receives the ball (B).
- 1 runs towards the 7-meter line while holding the ball and passes it into the running path of 4 (C) who approaches the goal dynamically.

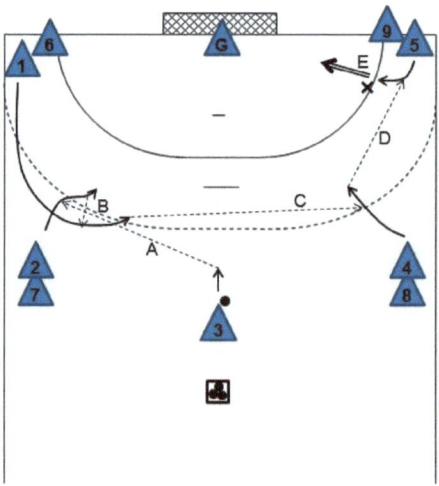

- 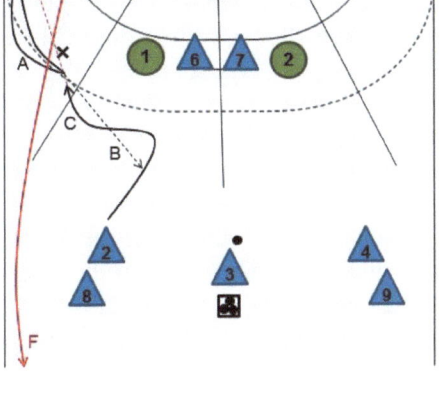 makes a piston movement towards the goal and plays a bounce pass to 5 (D) who shoots from the wing position (E).
- Afterwards, 1 and 2 switch positions.
- 3 starts the piston movement again and passes the ball to 8. Repeat the course on the other side.

No. 43	All-position shooting with defense	12	★★
Equipment required:	4 cones, ball box with sufficient number of handballs		

Setting:
- Use the cones to define the running paths on the wing position.

Basic course:
- The individual shots are to be thrown in short intervals.
- One defensive player per middle sector (preferably a back player and a pivot who switch regularly)
- All players must shoot from their respective position in the following order: left wing, pivot left, pivot right, left back, right back, right wing.
- Each pivot should shoot from both sides.

Course on the wing positions:
- 1 makes a piston movement on a curved path (A) and passes the ball to 2 who makes a piston movement towards the center (B).
- 2 feints a shot and then dynamically dribbles towards the wing position (C).

⚠ 2 must receive the pass in such a way that he does not have to dribble before feinting the shot.

- 2 passes the ball into the running path of 1 (D) who has immediately moved back to the wing position after playing the initial pass.
- 1 shoots at the goal (E), immediately runs a fast break, receives a pass from the goalkeeper G into his running path, and eventually shoots at the opposite goal (F).
- Afterwards, the next player starts the same course on the left wing position.

Course on the left back position for the pivot:

- ▲2 receives a pass from ▲3 into his running path (H).
- ●1 should clearly move towards the attacking player's movement (G).
- ▲2 should move towards the goal until he almost reaches ●1 and then pass the ball around ●1's body to the pivot (J).
- ▲6 leaves his starting position near the 7-meter line, picks up the ball, and eventually shoots at the goal (K).
- Repeat the course on the same side with ▲7.

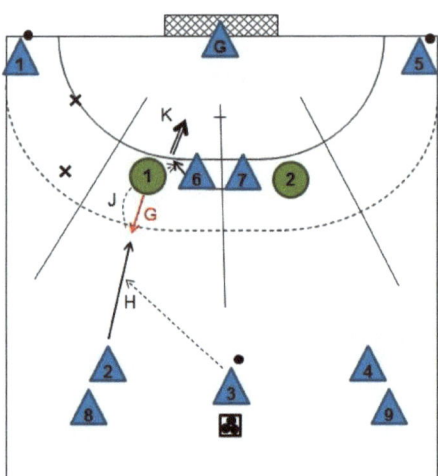

Course on the left back position for the back players:

- ▲2 makes a dynamic piston movement towards the left (M) and receives a pass into his running path (L).
- ●1 should clearly move towards ▲2's movement (N).
- ▲2 makes an extensive shooting feint (M).
- ▲6 leaves his starting position at the 7-meter line, moves forward along with ●1, and places a screen on the inner side (O).
- ▲2 dynamically runs (dribbles) to the inner side around the screening of ▲6, then approaches the goal (P), and eventually makes a jump shot from the 9-meter line (Q).
- Afterwards, it's the turn of the next back position player. Each player must do the course twice (two shots).

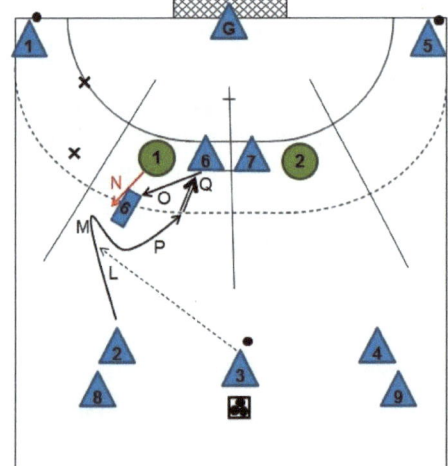

Repeat the course on the right side.

⚠ The individual courses should be performed quickly and without a break; the other players should not have to wait for too long.

Varied handball shooting drills
60 exercises for every handball training unit

No. 44	Shooting with consecutive 1-on-1 fast break	8	★★
Equipment required:	4 cones, 2 ball boxes with sufficient number of handballs		

Setting:
- Define two lines with cones.
- The players are given the numbers 1 to 3.

Course:

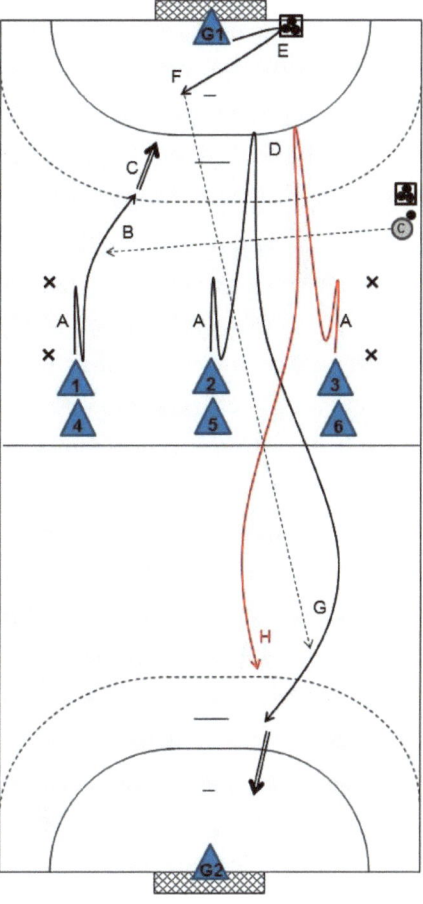

- 1, 2, and 3 simultaneously start to move forward and backward dynamically between the lines defined by the cones (A).
- While the players move, C calls out a number ("1" in the example).
- 1 starts approaching the goal immediately, receives a pass from C into his running path (B), and eventually shoots at the goal (C).
- When C calls out a number, the two other players (here 2 and 3) sprint towards the 6-meter line, put their foot on it, and start running a fast break immediately afterwards (D).
- After 1 has shot, G1 runs towards the ball box immediately, picks up a ball (E), and initiates the fast break. However, he must run a few meters to the side (F) in order to play a diagonal pass (G).
- G1 may choose to whom he wants to pass the ball (here 2). The other player becomes the defense player and tries to interrupt the fast break (H). If he manages to win the ball, he may try to score a goal himself.

⚠ The running moves should be done at top speed.

⚠ Make sure the players react immediately.

No. 45	Two shots over the block with consecutive fast break	10	★★
Equipment required:	Ball box with sufficient number of handballs		

Course:

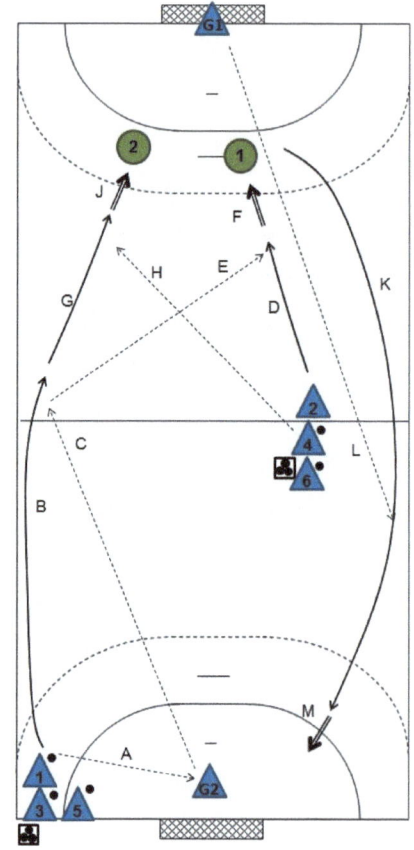

- ① passes the ball to the goalkeeper (A), starts running a fast break (B), and receives the ball from G2 (C).
- ② starts from the center line (D), receives a pass from ① into his running path (E), and shoots over ① who serves as defensive block (F).
- After he has played the pass, ① has slowed down, now speeds up again (G), receives a pass from ④ into his running path (H), and shoots over the defensive block of ② (J).
- During the shot of ① (J), ① starts running a fast break (K).
- G1 secures the ball and passes it into the running path of ① (L). ① eventually shoots at the goal (M).
- After serving as defensive block, ② takes over the position of ①. ② becomes the new block player and takes over the position of ②. ① lines up (with a ball) in the center behind ⑥. ① lines up (with a ball) behind ⑤, etc.

Variant:

- The players must play 1-on-1 against ① instead of shooting over the block.

⚠ The players should run a curve during their fast break so that they can catch the ball in an optimal way.

⚠ The block players should immediately start running their fast break during the second shot.

⚠ Change the side after a while.

Varied handball shooting drills
60 exercises for every handball training unit

| No. 46 | Shooting in the 1st wave with previous exercise | 5 | ★★ |

Equipment required: 2 small gym mats, 2 cones, ball box with sufficient number of handballs

Setting:
- Position two mats at the center line with one cone to the left and one to the right, i.e. on each 9-meter line.

Course:
- The two goals are named "North" and "South".
- 1 and 2 start doing jumping jacks on the gym mat while passing a ball (A).
- After a few passes, the coach calls out "North" or "South" ("North" in the example).
- The player holding the ball (here 1) starts dribbling towards the respective goal (B) immediately after the coach's command and shoots eventually (C).
- The other player (2) runs around the cone on the other side (D) and then starts running a fast break towards the respective goal (E).
- In the meantime, 3 passes a ball to the goalkeeper in the other goal (G2) (F).
- G2 goes into a good throwing position (G) (diagonal pass) and passes the ball into the running path of 2 (H) who eventually shoots at the goal (J).
- Immediately after the coach's command, the next two players start on the mats.

⚠ The players should react immediately after the coach's command and run in the correct direction.

⚠ Substitute 3 after 3 to 5 passes.

Varied handball shooting drills
60 exercises for every handball training unit

No. 47	Series of shots with undetermined situations	9	★★★
Equipment required:	4 cones, sufficient number of handballs		

Setting:
- Position cones as shown in the figure.

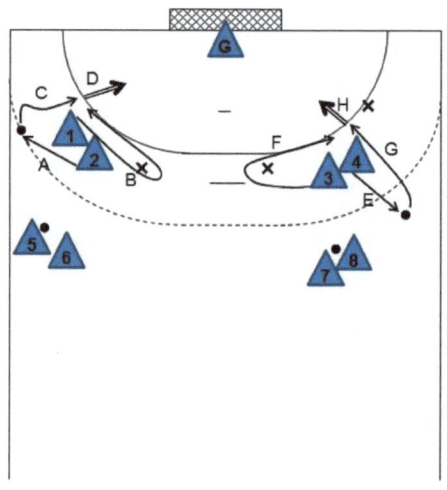

Course:
- The exercise is done on the left wing and the right back position alternately. Change the sides after several courses (right wing and left back).
- The players form pairs (change pairs during each course).
- The first pair puts their ball on the floor on the 9-meter line on the wing position. The players stand face-to-face between the 6- and 9-meter line and hold hands.
One player is assigned the color "black", the other one the color "white".
- The coach calls out "black" or "white".
- The respective player (here 2) runs towards the ball (A), picks it up, and approaches the goal (C).
- The other player (1) runs around the cone (B) and tries to slightly interfere with the shot of the first player (D).
- In the meantime, the first pair on the right back position has put their ball on the floor in front of the 9-meter line and chosen their colors, "black" or "white".
- Once again, the coach calls out "black" or "white", the respective player (4) fetches the ball (E), approaches the goal (G), and shoots (H). The other player (3) runs around the cone (F), confines the space for the attacking player's break-through, and slightly interferes with the shot.
- Afterwards, the next pair starts on the left wing position, etc.

⚠ In spite of the time pressure and the defending player's action, the attacking players should approach the goal at full speed, jump, and concentrate on the shot.

Variant:
- Instead of calling out "black" or "white", the coach calls out a word that is associated with the respective color (e.g., milk, cloud, coal, night, ...).

Varied handball shooting drills
60 exercises for every handball training unit

No. 48	Series of shots with coordination and passing exercise	8	★★★
Equipment required:	1 coordination ladder, 2 cones, ball box with sufficient number of handballs		

Setting:
- Put the coordination ladder on the floor and define the running path with cones (see figure).

Course:
- 1 starts without a ball and runs through the coordination ladder with two footsteps per interspace (left and right foot) (A).
- While 1 is running through the coordination ladder, he receives a ball from C (B) and passes it back to C (C).
- Once he has arrived at the end of the coordination ladder, 1 sprints around the cone (D), sprints back towards the backmost cone, again receives a ball from C (E), and passes it back (F).
- 1 runs around the second cone (G), sprints towards the goal (J), receives a ball from C (H), and eventually shoots at the goal (K).
- After he has shot (K), 1 starts a fast break immediately (L) and receives a new ball from C (M).
- Once he has crossed the center line, 1 passes the ball to 2, receives a return pass immediately (N), and eventually shoots at the goal (O).
- Afterwards, 2 lines up behind 4 and is substituted with 1 (P).
- After C has played the last pass to 1 (M), 3 starts the same drill, etc.

⚠ 1 should change directions quickly and dynamically.

⚠ 1 should play each return pass immediately after catching the ball.

No. 49	Series of shots with athletics drill and defense	9	★★★
Equipment required:	2 balance benches, 4 cones, ball box with sufficient number of handballs		

Setting:
- Position the benches and cones as shown in the figure.

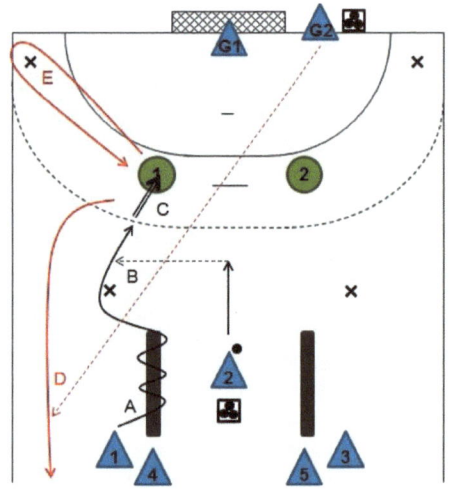

Basic course:
- Three players per side do the course alternately.
- Substitute ① and ② after three defense actions.

Course:
- ① starts the course and jumps over the bench with one leg (A) (landing and jumping with the right foot on the right side, landing and jumping with the left foot on the left side, etc.).
- After jumping over the bench, ① runs towards the cone on the left side. ① makes a parallel piston movement and passes the ball into the running path of his teammate (B).
- ① makes a jump shot over ① who serves as defensive block (C).
- Afterwards, ① starts a fast break immediately, receives a pass from the 2nd goalkeeper (or the coach) into his running path, and eventually shoots at the opposite goal (D).
- After he has served as defensive block, ① runs around the cone (E) and then waits for the next shot.

Repetitions:
- Each player does the drill (shot and fast break) 10 times counting his goals. Which shooter (which side) has scored most often after 10 drills? Define an exercise for the losers.

No. 50	Series of shots with four 1-on-1 actions	10	★★★
Equipment required:	3 cones, 1 handball per player		

Course:

- 1, 2, 3, and 4 start running a fast break simultaneously (A).
- The goalkeepers decide with their pass who becomes an attacking player (here: 1 and 3) and who becomes a defense player (here: 2 and 4) (B).
- The attacking players try to approach the goal 1-on-1 and shoot eventually. If the defense player wins the ball, he may shoot himself (at the same goal).

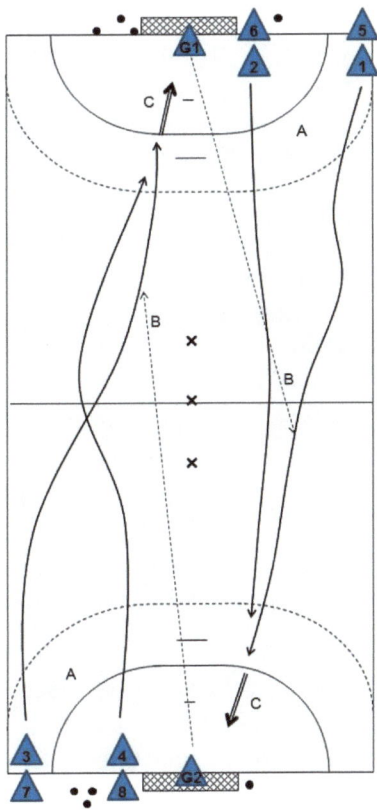

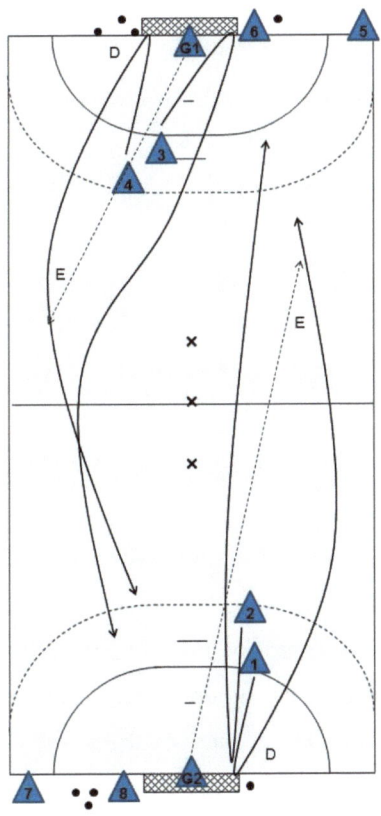

- Afterwards, the players sprint towards the goalpost, touch it, and start running the 2nd fast break (D).
- Again, the goalkeeper must decide to whom he wants to pass the ball (E). The players repeat the course on the other side.
- Afterwards, it is the next four players' turn.

⚠ The goalkeeper should vary his passes, i.e. pass the ball to the foremost player, to the backmost player, play a fast short pass, or a long-distance pass.

Category: Shooting competitions

No. 51	Shooting competition with game of pairs	9	★
Equipment required:	1 large vaulting box, 4 cones, 1 game of pairs, ball box with sufficient number of handballs		

Setting:
- Position a large vaulting box in the center of the court and put a game of pairs (8 to 10 pairs) upside down on top of the box.
- Make two teams.

Course 1: upper half
- The players of the first team line up in the center, each holding a handball except for the last player.
- 4 (the last player) starts without a ball, runs around the cone near the center line (A), then sprints quickly towards the goal, and receives a pass from 3 into his running path (B).
- 4 shoots from the left wing position (C).
- Afterwards, 3 starts doing the same course and receives a pass from 2.
- 4 lines up again in front of 1 and picks up a ball from the ball box.
- Once each player has shot from the left wing position, the course starts over on the right side, then on the left side again, etc.

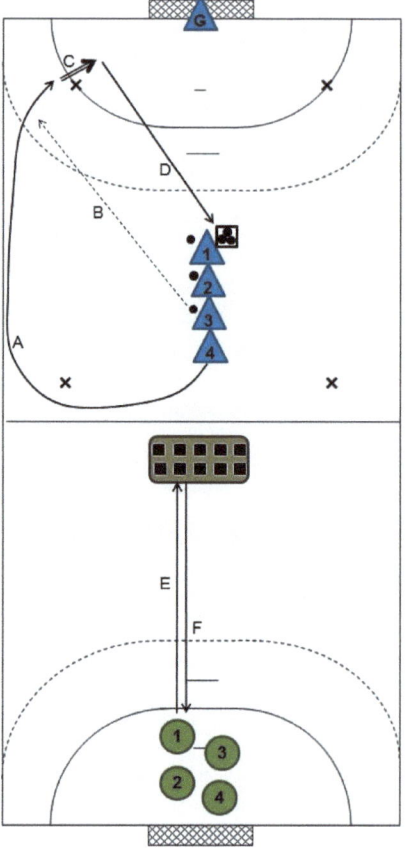

Course 2: bottom half
- The second team starts from the goal zone.
- 1 runs towards the vaulting box and flips two cards of the game of pairs (E).
- If the cards match, 1 takes them with him to the group; if the cards do not match, 1 flips them back and runs back leaving the cards on the box (F).
- 1 exchanges a high-five with the next player who then repeats the course, etc.

Varied handball shooting drills
60 exercises for every handball training unit

Overall course:
- The team in the upper half may shoot until the second team has finished the game of pairs.
- Afterwards, they switch tasks.
- Which team has shot the most goals?

⚠ During the game of pairs, the players should communicate in order to finish it quickly.

No. 52	Shooting competition with medicine balls	6	★
Equipment required:	4 cones, 5 medicine balls, 1 handball per player		

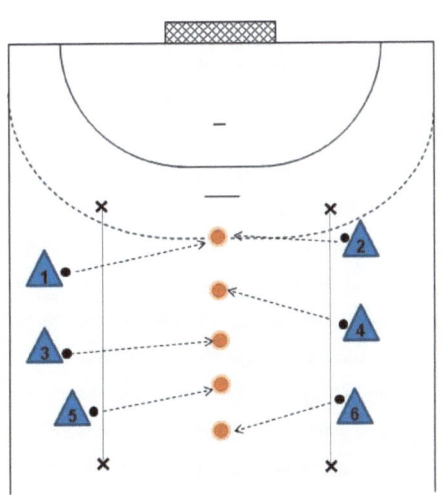

Setting:
- Define two lines with cones (or use existing lines).
- The players are divided into two teams. Each player has a handball.
- The teams stand behind the lines (one team per side).
- Put medicine balls on the floor between the defined lines.

Course:
- On command, both teams start and try to move the medicine balls across the opponents' line by aiming and shooting their handballs at the medicine balls.
- The players may all shoot at the same time and at all the medicine balls.
- Once a medicine ball has crossed one of the lines completely, the players must not shoot at this medicine ball anymore.
- Which team has moved the most medicine balls into the opponents' playing field in the end?

⚠ Adjust the distance between the lines and the medicine balls to the players' level of performance.

Varied handball shooting drills
60 exercises for every handball training unit

No. 53	Shooting competition with dices	7	★
Equipment required:	6 simple cones, 6 cones in different colors, 1 foam dice, 1 handball		

Setting:
- Define three shooting zones using four cones and assign them the numbers 1, 2, and 3.
- Make two teams. For each team, define a line with three cones in different colors. Put another cone near the center line (see figure).
- Put a dice on the floor at the center line and a handball on the floor between the two playing fields.

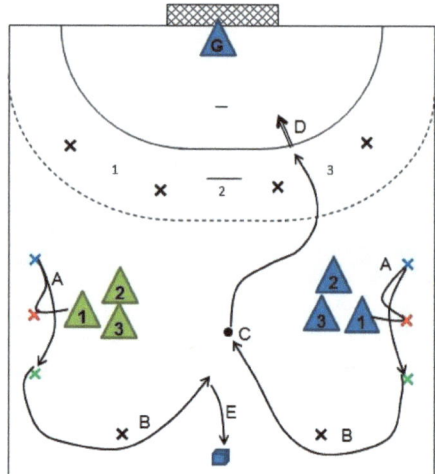

Course:
- The coach calls various cone colors (in the figure, "red", "blue", and "green").
- 🔺 and 🔺 run towards the cones and touch them in the correct order (A) while always facing the side line.
- After the coach has called out the colors, he calls out "1", "2", or "3", which is the sign for 🔺 and 🔺 to run around the backmost cone (B) and then try to win the handball lying on the floor between the two playing fields (C). In the figure, 🔺 wins the ball.
- The player who has won the ball (🔺) runs through the respective corridor ("3" in the example) and shoots at the goal (D).
- The other player (🔺) runs towards the dice and rolls it once (E).
- If 🔺 hits the goal, he gets the number of points on the dice; if 🔺 misses the goal, the other team gets the points.
- Afterwards, put a new handball on the floor and the next two players start the drill.
- Which team has scored highest in the end?

⚠ The players should do the running moves between the cones quickly. However, when the coach calls out a number, they should react immediately and start the second part of the drill.

Varied handball shooting drills
60 exercises for every handball training unit

No. 54	Shooting competition timed by the other group 1	9	★
Equipment required:	6 poles, 2 small gym mats, 10 cones, 1 balance bench, ball box with sufficient number of handballs		

Setting:
- Position the poles, gym mats, cones, and the balance bench as shown in the figure.

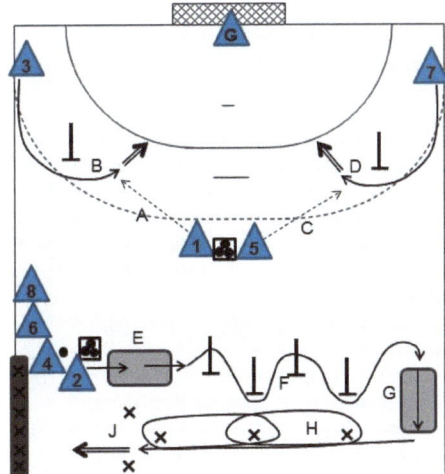

Course of team 1:
- 3 starts on the wing position, runs a curve around the pole, receives a ball from 1 into his running path (A), and shoots (B).
- Afterwards, the course starts over on the other side (C and D).
- After the wing players have shot (B and D), they move on and become the feeding players. Once the previous feeding players have played the pass (A and C), they move on and become the wing players.

Course of team 2:
- 2 starts and does 10 quick jumping jacks on the mat while holding a handball (E).
- Afterwards, 2 sidesteps quickly around the poles while holding the handball over his head (F).
- 2 does a somersault on the mat (G).
- Afterwards, 2 runs around the second cone, around the first cone, around the third cone, around the second cone, and towards the third cone again (H). While running, he dribbles the ball.
- 2 shoots from between the two cones and tries to hit one of the cones on the bench (J).
- As soon as 2 does the somersault on the mat (G), 4 starts the course.
- After he has shot, 2 lines up again.

Overall course:
- Team 2 repeats the course until no cones are left on the bench. Team 1 may shoot at the goal until team 2 has hit all the cones.
- Afterwards, the teams switch tasks.
- Which team has shot the most goals?

Overall course variant:
- Set the time (e.g. to 10 minutes). Team 1 gets a point for each goal; team 2 gets a point for each cone they hit (always put the cones back on the bench).
- Afterwards, the teams switch tasks and try to score during the other part of the drill.

Which team has scored highest?

No. 55	Shooting competition timed by the other group 2	9	★★
Equipment required:	2 large safety mats, 2 small vaulting boxes, 1 balance bench, 4 cones, ball box with sufficient number of handballs		

Setting:
- Define the starting points with cones in the upper half of the court, as shown in the figure.
- Put two large safety mats, two small vaulting boxes, a balance bench, and two cones on the floor in the bottom half of the court, as shown in the figure.
- Make two teams.

Course of team 1 (upper half):
- 2 dribbles towards the cone (A) and passes the ball to 1 (B).
- 2 starts crossing (C) and receives a pass from 1 into his running path (D).
- 1 takes on the crossing (E), receives the ball (F), and shoots at the goal (G).
- After the crossing, 2 moves back to the initial position of 1 (H).
- By the time 1 is shooting, 3 starts dribbling towards the cone and the course starts over.

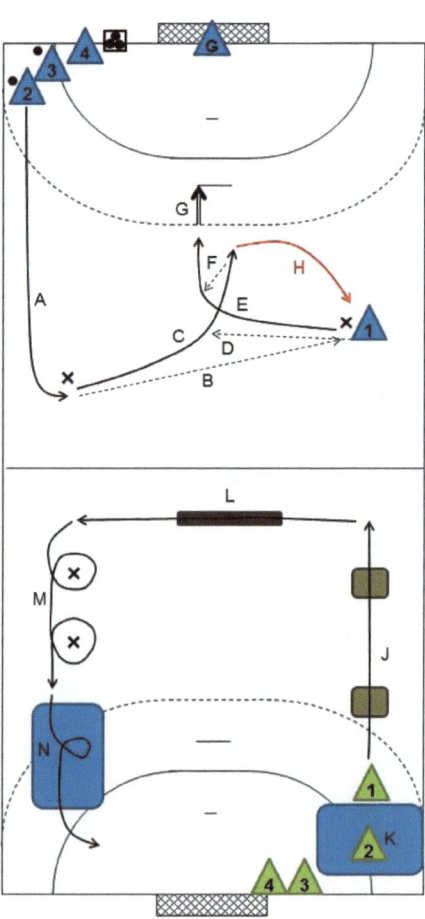

Course of team 2 (bottom half):

- 1 starts and crosses the two small vaulting boxes (jump on the box with both legs and step down) (J).
- Afterwards, 1 runs towards the balance bench, lies face-down, and pulls himself to the other side using both arms (L).
- 1 runs around both cones completely (M) and finally does a forward somersault on the large safety mat (N).
- While 1 is doing the course, 2 does jumping jacks on the other large safety mat (K).
- Once 1 has entered the goal zone, this is the sign for 2 (running course) and 3 (jumping jacks on the mat) to start.

Overall course:

- Count the goals of team 1.
- Team 1 may shoot at the goal until each player of team 2 has done the course six (ten) times.
- Afterwards, the teams switch tasks.

Which team has shot the most goals?

No. 56	Shooting at fixed targets vs. shooting at the goal	9	★★
Equipment required:	8 cones, 2 small vaulting boxes, 1 large vaulting box, foam dices, 2 ball boxes with sufficient number of handballs		

Setting:

- Make two teams.
- Define the running paths towards the goal using cones.
- For the second team, define the starting point with a cone, define the shooting line, and position two small vaulting boxes with foam dices (or medicine balls) on top and a large vaulting box with three cones on top (see figure).

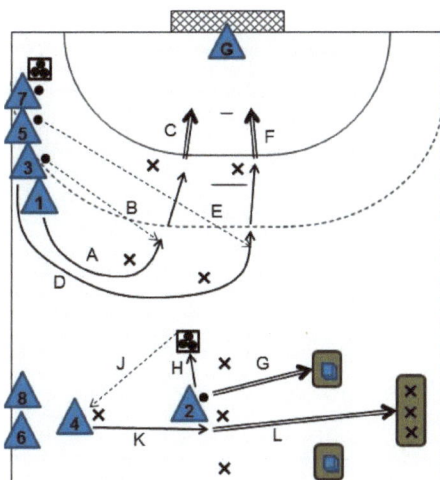

Course of team 1:

- ▲1 starts without a ball and runs a curve around the first cone in the back (A). Once he has run around the cone, he receives the ball from ▲3 (B), approaches the goal, and shoots (C).
- After the shot, ▲3 runs around the second cone in the back (D), receives a pass from ▲5 into his running path (E), and shoots (F).
- Afterwards, ▲5 starts the same course and receives a pass from ▲7 (not shown in the figure).
- The players should line up in such a way that they shoot and pass and run the long and the short way towards the goal alternately.

Course of team 2:

- ▲2 starts at the shooting line and shoots at one of the targets (G).
- When hitting a target, the players get points as follows:
    - Hitting the dice: The team gets the number of points shown on the dice.
    - Hitting a cone on top of the large vaulting box: The team gets 5 points.
- After he has shot, ▲2 runs to the ball box (H) and passes a ball to ▲4 (J).
- ▲4 runs towards the shooting line (K) and shoots (L).
- And so on.

Overall course:

- Team 2 may try to collect points until team 1 has shot 15 goals.
- Switch tasks afterwards.
- Which team has scored highest in the end?

⚠ If no foam dice is available, the players may shoot at a cone or a medicine ball instead. Once they have hit the respective target, the team may roll a small dice to figure out the number of points.

Varied handball shooting drills
60 exercises for every handball training unit

No. 57	Shooting biathlon	10	★★
Equipment required:	12 cones, 10 handballs		

Setting:
- Make two teams.
- For each team, put five handballs on the floor along the 9-meter line as shown in the figure and position cones to define the running path and the "penalty round".

Course:
- On command, 🔺1 and 🔺1 start simultaneously and run around the first cone (A).
- 🔺1 and 🔺1 run a slalom around the three cones (B), run towards the first ball, pick it up (C), and shoot (D).
- Afterwards, 🔺1 and 🔺1 run back towards the three cones (E), repeat the slalom run, and pick up the next ball.
- The players repeat the drill until no handballs are left.
- For each missed shot, 🔺1 and 🔺1 must run a penalty round around the two cones in center afterwards (F).
- As soon as there is no handball left, 🔺4 and 🔺4 put new handballs on the floor.
- Following the last penalty round, the next shooter may start.
- 🔺1 and 🔺1 take over the position of 🔺4 and 🔺4, respectively. 🔺4 and 🔺4 line up behind the shooters.
- Which team has shot the most goals within the defined time period?

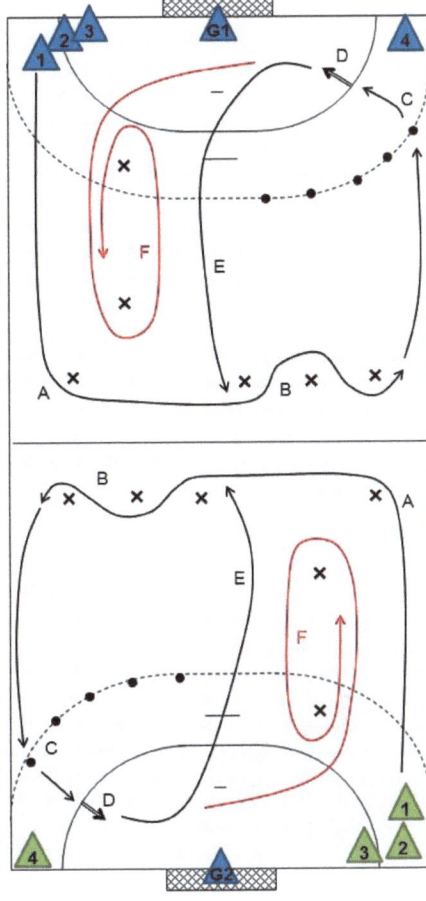

⚠️ The teams should not be too large so that the players do not have to wait for too long. For larger groups, the waiting player starts immediately after the last shot. The previous player runs his penalty rounds in parallel.

| No. 58 | Fast break shooting competition | 8 | ★★ |

Equipment required: 8 cones, 1 handball per player

Course:

- 1 and 1 start simultaneously and dribble towards the other side (A).
- Once they have arrived, they shoot at the goal from between the first two cones (B).
- If the player scores a goal (1 in the figure), he fetches his ball, dribbles back, and, once he has crossed the center line (C), passes the ball to the next player of his group (D).
- If the player misses the goal (1 in the figure), he fetches his ball, dribbles towards the center line (E), and may try again. This time, he shoots from the center however (F). Afterwards, he fetches his ball, dribbles towards the center line (G), and passes the ball to the next player of his group (H) (even if he missed the second time, too).
- Once the next player has caught the pass, he starts the drill.

Competition:
- Count the goals of each team.
- Which team has scored highest within the defined time period?

⚠ Once they have shot, the players should fetch their ball immediately and either start their second try or pass the ball to the next player.

⚠ The goalkeepers might be switched after the first half of the playing time.

⚠ For a smaller group, consider allowing a third shooting try from between the third and fourth cone before passing the ball to the next player.

| No. 59 | Shooting competition focusing on endurance | 8 | ★★★ |

| Equipment required: | 6 cones, sufficient number of handballs |

Setting:
- Position cones as shown in the figure.

Basic course:
- Make two teams.
- Two players (one player of each team) do the course.
- The other players jog at relaxed pace around the cones in the center (A).

Course:
- 1 and 2 stand on the wing position and start to run a fast break simultaneously.
- The goalkeepers each play a long pass (B).
- 1 and 2 each shoot at the goal (C).
- After they have shot, both players sprint to the goal and touch one of the goalposts (D).
- Afterwards, they start a second fast break, receive a long pass from the respective goalkeeper into their running paths (E), and eventually shoot at the goal (F).
- The player who shot the most goals scores for his team. If there is a tie, both teams score.
- 1 and 2 then join the jogging players in the center. Two new players start the same course.

- Each player must do the course twice (i.e. shoot 4 times); the final score will be settled at the end. The losing team must do push-ups or sit-ups, for example.

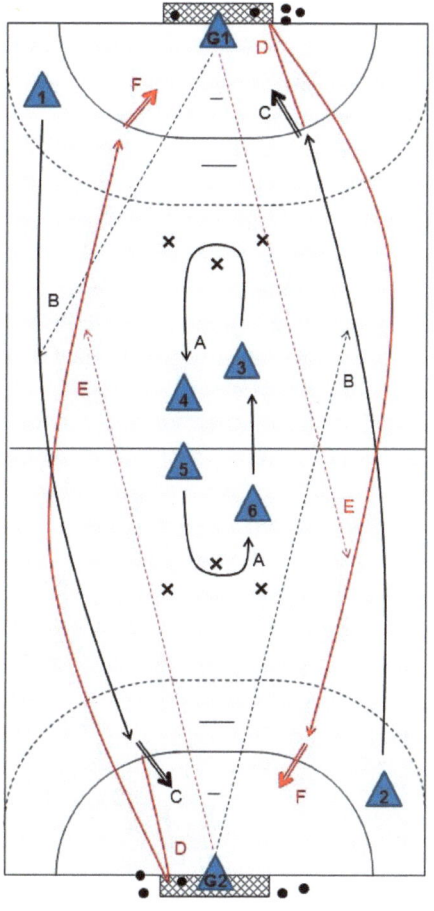

Varied handball shooting drills
60 exercises for every handball training unit

No. 60	Sprint-and-shoot relay race with dices	12	★★★
Equipment required:	6 cones, 2 dices, 2 ball boxes with two handballs each		

Setting:
- Two teams stand as shown in the figure, each with a dice and a ball box containing two handballs.

Course:
- On command, both teams start the course in parallel.
- 1 and 1 roll the dice (A), run to the ball box, pick up a ball (B), and shoot at the goal from the 9-meter line (C).
- If the dice shows an even number, they may only shoot once. If the dice shows an uneven number, they run back to the ball box, pick up a second ball, and shoot at the goal once again.
- After the shot/the two shots, the players must put the balls back into the ball box first.
- If they hit the goal with each shot, they run around the cone and back to their team immediately (E) and the next player starts the drill (F).
- For each missed shot, the shooter must run around the two cones once (G) and afterwards sprint back until he arrives at the other cone (H).
- The players of which team manage to complete the drill once (twice) first?

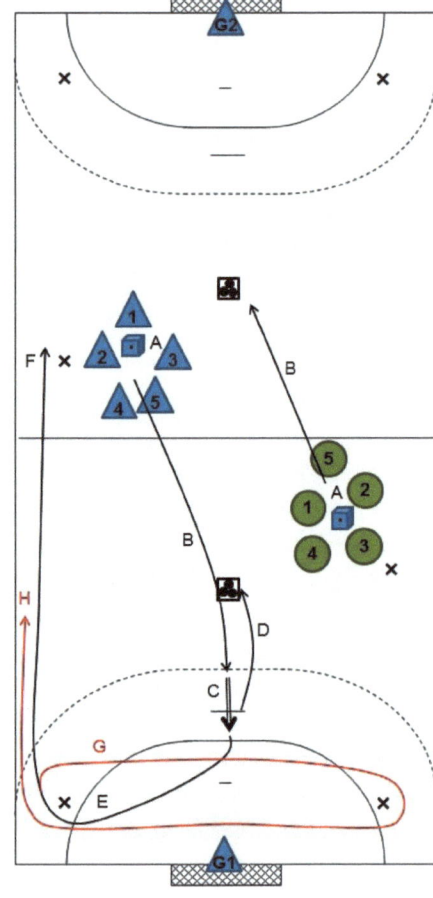

⚠️ If the dice shows 1, 3, or 5: shoot once. If the dice shows 2, 4, or 6: shoot twice.

⚠️ If the player scored once/twice: run back immediately (F). If the player missed once: run around the cones once (G). If the player missed twice: run around the cones twice (G).

Editor's note

JÖRG MADINGER, born in Heidelberg (Germany) in 1970

July 2014 (further training): 3-day coaching workshop: "Basic components of goalkeeper training", held by the German Handball Association (Deutscher Handballbund, DHB)
Lecturers: Michael Neuhaus, Renate Schubert, Marco Stange, Norbert Potthoff, Olaf Gritz, Andreas Thiel, Henning Fritz

May 2014 (further training): 3-day coaching further training during the VELUX EHF Final4, held by the **German Handball Coaching Association (Deutsche Handball Trainer Vereinigung, DHTV)/DHB**
Lecturers: Jochen Beppler (DHB coach), Christian vom Dorff (DHB referee), Mark Dragunski (coach of TuSeM Essen, Germany),
Klaus-Dieter Petersen (DHB coach), Manolo Cadenas (coach of the Spanish national team)

May 2013 (further training): 3-day coaching further training during the VELUX EHF Final4, held by the **German Handball Coaching Association (Deutsche Handball Trainer Vereinigung, DHTV)/DHB**
Lecturers: Prof. Dr. Carmen Borggrefe (University of Stuttgart, Germany), Klaus-Dieter Petersen (DHB coach), Dr. Georg Froese (sports psychologist), Jochen Beppler (DHB base camp coach), Carsten Alisch (young talents' hockey coach)

Since July 2012: A-License, DHB

Since February 2011: Handball club trainings, coaching (training and competitive areas)

November 2011: Foundation of the Handball Specialist Publishing Company (Handball Fachverlag) (handball-uebungen.de, Handball Practice and Special Handball Practice)

May 2009: Foundation of the handball online platform handball-uebungen.de

2008-2010: Youth coordinator and youth coach, SG Leutershausen (Germany)

Since 2006: B-License

Editor's note

In 1995, a friend convinced me to join him in coaching a handball youth team (male, under 13 years of age).

This was the beginning of my career as a team handball coach. Ever since I enjoyed working as a coach and had high requirements concerning my exercises. Soon, the standard pool of exercises wasn't enough for me anymore and I started to modify and develop drills myself.

Today, I coach a broad range of youth and adult teams with different performance levels and adjust my training units to the individual needs of the teams.

A few years ago, I started selling my exercises and drills online at handball-uebungen.de. Since, in handball training, there is a tendency towards a general athletic training that focuses on coordination work – especially in the training of youth teams –, a large number of my games and exercises can be applied to other sports as well.

Get inspired by the various game concepts, be creative, and rely on your own experiences!

Yours sincerely,
Jörg Madinger

Further reference books published by DV Concept

From warm-up to handball team play – 75 exercises for every handball training unit

By making your training units more diverse, you can increase the players' motivation, since you consistently offer new approaches to improve and refine familiar movement sequences. In this book, you will find inspiring exercises you can apply during each phase of your everyday team handball training – from warm-up and goalkeeper warm-up shooting to the common contents of the main phase and the closing games. Each exercise is illustrated and described in an easy, comprehensible manner. Specific notes give you tips on what you need to be aware of.

This book deals with the following key subjects:

Warm-up:
- Basic warm-up
- Short warm-up games
- Sprint contests
- Coordination
- Ball familiarization
- Goalkeeper warm-up shooting

Basic exercises, basic play, and target play:
- Offense/series of shots
- General offense
- Fast throw-off
- 1st and 2nd wave
- Defensive action
- Closing games
- Endurance

At the end of this book, you will find an entire methodological training unit. The objective of this training unit is to improve shooting and quick decision-making under pressure.

For further reference and e-books visit us at:
www.handball-uebungen.de

www.ingramcontent.com/pod-product-compliance
Lightning Source LLC
Chambersburg PA
CBHW041803160426
43191CB00001B/21